The Thoughtful Girl's Guide

to FASHION, COMMUNICATION, and FRIENDSHIP

The Thoughtful Girl's Guide

to FASHION, COMMUNICATION, and FRIENDSHIP

MARY SHEEHAN WARREN

TAN Books

Charlotte, North Carolina

Cover and interior design by Caroline K. Green
Cover image by Dean Drobot/ShutterStock

Library of Congress Control Number: 2018956441

ISBN: 978-1-5051-1124-8

Published in the United States by
TAN Books
PO Box 410487
Charlotte, NC 28241
www.TANBooks.com

Printed in the United States of America

For Maryclare, Gracie, and Lilly.

And for Gerry and William.

Contents

INTRODUCTION
Is that You? xi

CHAPTER 1
What's So Me? *Knowing the Subject Matters*. 1

CHAPTER 2
Listen to Me: *Listening and Speaking*. 29

CHAPTER 3
Look at That: *The Possibilities of Fashion* 67

CHAPTER 4
Look at Me! *Personal Fashion Choices*. 95

CHAPTER 5
Leaving my Mark: *Media Literacy* 141

CHAPTER 6
See What I Mean? *Virtue and Manners*. 177

EPILOGUE
Understanding in a World of Misunderstanding. 211

Sources and Suggestions for Further Reading 215

Photo Credits 219

Acknowledgments

My first and warmest thank-you is to my husband: *Thank you for understanding me, Robert.*

I also thank Mary Anne Wahle, Jeannette Kendall, and Patti Francomacaro for being so helpful both personally and professionally. A very big thank you goes also to my mentor, Margery Sinclair, and my "big sisters" Joana Allan and Mary Demet. Thanks to Maureen Bielinski for checking over the philosophical underpinnings of my first chapter and Rose Haas and Liz Brach for their moral support and encouragement. Thanks also to Maryclare Warren, Grace Warren, Lilly Warren, Madeline Haas, Anne Marie Haas, Christina Sheehan, "Little" Mary Sheehan, Katie Rose, Lilly Sheehan, Margaret Brach, Lucia Brach, Sarah Brach, Rosie Brach, and even little Lizzie Brach for giving me a vision for why I am writing this book in the first place. Thanks also to Tom Spence for encouraging me, Father Jack Kubik for teaching me, and John Moorehouse for entrusting me with this awesome task.

Author's Note

This is a book for women, especially young women. Most of the material presented *could* have been relevant to men, but the core message is tailored so specifically to the feminine soul, that in the end, *none* of its material is relevant to men.

Is That You?

Imagine this brief conversation between you and an acquaintance at a bus stop along a busy street:

"That is so you!" she says.
"What's so me?" you ask.
"That. Your whole look; what you're wearing, I mean."

Her words would grab your attention, wouldn't they? Your initial reaction would be to smile and think that *yes, I dress to express the real "me" in my fashion.*

But let's say that with the final line, she hops onto her bus and leaves you alone with your thoughts. This is when you might begin to wonder:

Was that a sort of compliment?
Or was it a put-down in disguise?
What is it about how I look today that's so me *and how would she know anyway?*
What is she saying about my taste? About my choices? About me as a person?

SO YOU, SO ME,

So what?

It's fair to say that something out there is "so you" while many other things aren't. You know it's not literal, of course, and you are sophisticated enough to realize that an appearance doesn't define you or give you an *identity* in the true sense of the word. On the other hand, you've subconsciously operated on the idea that a physical appearance, especially an entire outfit, can contribute to an identity—or, really, a subjective *feeling* of that identity. So, yes, fashion is a pretty powerful thing and maybe you would be right to get all prickly about your friend's comment.

We tend to have a lot of angst about how we look in the eyes of others even when we say we aren't. (Or, *especially* when we say we aren't!) It's a funny question to consider, but how is it that we can spend a lifetime glancing in mirrors, studying ourselves in photographs, and listening to ourselves speak only to *never completely know how we look, how we sound, or even who we are?*

Of course, when pressed with the question *"who are you?"* most of us can get beyond how we think we appear to others and, perhaps, mention the roles we have, the things we like, or the beliefs we keep. That's because we know, deep down in our bones, that there is a lot more to us than what meets the eye.

MORE THAN WHAT MEETS THE EYE

That's why this book covers more than fashion.

In my work as a small-business owner, a fashion stylist, and now a marketing lecturer to college students, I've spent a lot of time talking about appearances. My first book, *It's So You! Fitting Fashion to Your Life*, summarizes everything I learned about appearances during the first twenty years of my career. This knowledge informs me in my current work with Success In Style, a nonprofit organization dedicated to providing career apparel and professional presence skills to men and women in need.[1] To my great delight, the book has also helped many of my clients and friends and nowadays I meet women who have grown up on my ideas of color choice, wardrobe design, and *Barbie*.

However, since its publication a dozen years ago, I've noticed two new trends. First, there has been a revolution in our understanding of *appearances* because of our newer methods of communication. Second, because of this new understanding, each of us—now more than ever—needs to understand what exactly an appearance (or communication) is supposed to accomplish in the first place.

Keeping up the new appearance

That acquaintance at the bus stop? She also may have seen on social media what you wore last weekend, where you went, and with whom you went there. Depending upon how much you or your friends (or anyone else) have shared on the Internet, she may know what you had for breakfast, who your family is, what you think of the President, how you've donated your money, or where you're headed next weekend. In fact, in addition to any one person

....

[1] Success In Style was founded on the idea that since there is such a great dignity in human work, there must be a sort of "sacred space" for men and women to get what they need to be successful. See www.successinstyle.org.

at the bus stop, there is an unlimited number of people who have an unlimited access to the bits and bytes of that "appearance" otherwise known as *you*.

Social media is enchanting, almost magical. Using any number of platforms, I can create and control an ideal self that leads others to think the best about me. That seems innocent enough, doesn't it? What's the harm in a little sharing? What if my virtual self makes others happy? What if a little pretending is just another form of *faking it until making it*?

The best way to answer this question is to consider how we feel when we experience another person's specially crafted ideal self in social media. When we detect a disconnect between the real and the virtual, we can't help but feel a bit deceived. It's a feeling much like the one we have when we realize that an advertising image has been photoshopped, because we realize that the image is a fake and the message is a lie.

No fake news here

Our senses should help us get at the truth about the world around us. The smell of smoke should warn us about fire and a darkening sky should compel us to get an umbrella. On any city street, a business person's well-cut suit speaks of professionalism in a way that the tourist's shorts and sandals don't. Appearances, in the case of the human person, matter because they communicate about the communicator.

This book is a practical guide for communicating the truth about yourself. Although I've begun with a lesson on appearances, it would be silly to stay on that level only. The things we love about life—friendship, adventure, happiness, true-love—are fully realized once we get past the one-dimensional—but still very real—level of appearances.

In the first chapter, ***Knowing the Subject Matters***, we'll consider the some*thing* that is communicated, the heart and soul of the message.

The second chapter, ***Listening and Speaking***, is a study of spoken language, the most direct but sometimes most emotionally charged form of communication.

Chapters 3, ***The Possibilities of Fashion***, and 4, ***Personal Fashion Choices***, decode the signs and symbols of fashion so that our communication is clear and consistent in any situation.

And, Chapter 5, ***Media Literacy***, addresses how we are processing a lot of information very quickly and under less-than-ideal circumstances. But this chapter has also been included because even in this world of constant visual impression, we are now leaving a written record of ourselves more than ever before.

Finally, Chapter 6, ***Virtues and Manners***, will wrap it all up by offering a way to think about the intent, tone, and timing of any communication on any platform and at any time.

So, take out a sharpened pencil, cuddle up in cozy spot, and dig into a life-changing exploration of a fascinating topic: your own ways of communicating!

CHAPTER 1

What's So Me?

Knowing the Subject Matters

Think back to the *last* time someone misunderstood you. If you can't, perhaps this little real-world scenario will spark your memory:

After what Fanny Price thought was a great interview with her boss about a possible promotion in her part-time job at a clothing store, she found out later that she not only didn't get the position, but wasn't even on the list of finalists. When she timidly asked her boss about it, he said that he "had the impression" Fanny didn't think the new position would be worth it.

So, Fanny, as you can imagine, tried to recall the conversation to figure out how in the world she "gave the impression" she thought the job wasn't worth it?

Was that man listening to what I was saying? Did he miss something I said? Did I miss something he said? Who wasn't paying attention?

These are relevant questions because for communication to start, there must first be a connection. This is otherwise known as *getting attention*, *holding attention*, or *tuning in*. If you aren't tuned in, you don't get the program.

Fortunately, Fanny was mature enough to reflect:

What did I actually say? Did I forget to say something I was supposed to say?

And this is where we come to the heart of the matter: *saying something is more than talking*. (Of course, any one of us can mess talking up too.) Our desires, intentions, opinions, aspirations, attitudes, and even our sense of self-worth are each communicated by more than words. We reveal things about ourselves with our tone of voice, our facial expressions, our body language, and even the clothing we're wearing.

It's a cycle rather than just a chain of events because once two people understand each other, they reconnect in a stronger way and communicate on a deeper level. That's pretty powerful stuff! When the cycle is broken (there's no initial connection or communication is garbled), neither person understands anything coming from the other. And, sometimes, the other person (boss or teacher or coworker or friend) didn't just get the facts wrong; she got *you* wrong too!

If you don't know yourself all that well, couldn't it be possible that you don't know others as well as you've assumed? Are you in any position to guess why a person acts or speaks in a certain way? So, why do we make sweeping generalizations about people whom we barely know?

She's pretty, but probably doesn't have much depth to her.

There goes another over-protective mother who has nothing else better to do with her time.

He's just an obnoxious showoff who thinks he's hot stuff.

Can a person's life be summarized in a string of words?

No way. Nor, for that matter, could a paragraph, a book, or even a documentary film give justice as a record of a person's life narrative and inner world. We make blanket statements about people all the time because it's the easiest way to order the universe. The fact that we mentally categorize people in this way helps explain how your acquaintance at the bus stop might presume to suggest that an outfit is "so you." Don't *you* mentally sum up other people all the time?

You and I both label, categorize and pigeon-hole others as if we possessed an all-knowing presence much like the narrator in a long and rambling novel. Hopefully, as we learn about the world and listen to the concerns of others, we come to see that any other human being is not a one-dimensional character in a book and that:

A person is a person just like me. She can't know me without my help and I can't know her without hers.

But people can frustrate us. Sometimes, when we are angry, overwhelmed, or just baffled, we comfort ourselves with simple answers to questions such as:

Why does she always get what she wants?

Why does she always argue with me?

Why does he lie so often?

Why is she always smiling?

Why does he take such huge risks?

You dismiss the friend who has lied to you as a "liar" and the smiling friend as "out of it." In a similar way, you breezily guess that one friend's over-the-top humor is motivated by a desire to be popular, and that another's is driven by a cold detachment from caring what others may think. Then, you store those thoughts away like a thin, neat file filed into the ever-expanding filing cabinet section of your brain, referring to it every time you need an explanation for someone's annoying behavior or strange luck or seemingly undeserved successes. Your file may be a wholly inadequate explanation, but you like having the files. You like the order, the simplicity, and the apparent ability to file your friends in the first place. Ultimately, however, this filing cabinet ends up becoming a cold metal chamber of stereotypes.

Guessing about the interior life of another person may account for a person's behavior on a superficial level, or may even explain much of a person's actions, but you'll find out rather quickly that your fellow human being is a bit more complex. (Just like you are complex.) Your friend's truest thoughts, most treasured desires, and even her ultimate goals are a mystery to you—and maybe even to herself as well.

So now you are wondering, "why bother?" *Why bother to understand others if instead of a neat filing system, it's all one big puzzle?*

That puzzle you're stressing over is actually a *gift*. Perhaps, at times, a puzzling gift, but still a gift. While a puzzle is something you "solve" to see a predetermined, one-dimensional picture, a gift, on the other hand, is multi-dimensional, layered, valuable, freely given, actively received, and, under normal circumstances, benefits both the giver and the receiver. A gift requires gracious patience, especially when it must be unwrapped slowly. And a gift certainly calls for an attitude of gratitude that it is *present* in the first place. Friendship is the way we unwrap the "gift of person" so that we eventually understand what's inside: *first you get through that decorative ribbon, then a good tear at the tape, a pull at the paper, and finally an opening of a lid*. At the end of the unwrapping, you get a friend who remains a gift. And that gift can keep on giving.

And if you are following me closely here, you'll realize that if she's a gift, you are a gift as well.

You can't control how another person comes wrapped, and you certainly can't control the nature of her gift of self. You can, however, control all the signs and signals (the bows, the tape, the wrapping paper) on your own gift of self so that there is a genuine connection between what others first see about you and what they eventually understand about you (i.e., yourself as gift). This is *authenticity*, and it attracts true friends in deeper, longer-lasting relationships.

Even at our most authentic, it is fair to say that one of the greatest joys in life is finding a friend who unwraps you in a way that helps you to know and understand yourself.

What's an interior life?

A good friend (as well as a mom, a dad, or a mentor) can help you understand yourself only if you maintain your *capacity* to understand. Just like in the practical meaning of the word, it's a sort of space that's already inside you (so, the first word *interior*). If you clutter this space up with random stuff, the really good things—like knowledge of self and others, an instinct for the needs of others, gratitude, awe, peace, joy, and a sense of purpose—can't get in.

What's the stuff that can clutter up this space? Well, some stuff is good and can be used as hooks for hanging those truly good things onto: memories of kindness and compassion, hard-earned lessons, enriching stories, knowledge, planning, creative thinking, and even your genius ideas! But some stuff is no better than nasty, needless junk: images from entertainment and social media, random scenes from your own history, regrets, temptations, guilt, even past unkind exchanges and "ear worms."

The best way to keep this space free and clear of especially the bad stuff is to maintain some periods of silence. Unplug the earbuds, turn off the screen, stow away the phone, and relax your brain for a few moments every day and as often as you can. A real interior life begins with this sort of silence and should lead to the deliberate reflection on that good stuff I mentioned above. Many people pray during this time, and that's where the second part of the term, *life*, comes from. That silent, reflective time for people who pray can become a real and lively connection with God.

A GIFT ON A MISSION

Think about the person who can explain her reasons for doing what she does, living the way she lives, consistently saying the things she says. It's a rare thing, isn't it?

Young and Old: *Who can explain her own mission for life? You've probably never heard of either of the women above, but, even in their quiet lives, they understood their personal missions. Montse (left) was spirited, generous, and always trying to live according to her faith. Cancer struck her early in life and she lived cheerfully through terrible pain, remaining a friend to all she knew. She died at the age of 18, leaving an amazing legacy of love despite her short time on earth. Letty (right) lived a long life, raised six children (her seventh died as a baby), and still had time for her friends, neighbors, and siblings. Older people I know still tell "Letty Stories," so her influence continues despite her lack of fame or fortune.*

Now consider the question for yourself: what motivates *you*?

What gets you out of bed in the morning? What gets you through your typical day? What helps you survive a bad day? These aren't the easiest questions to answer, are they?

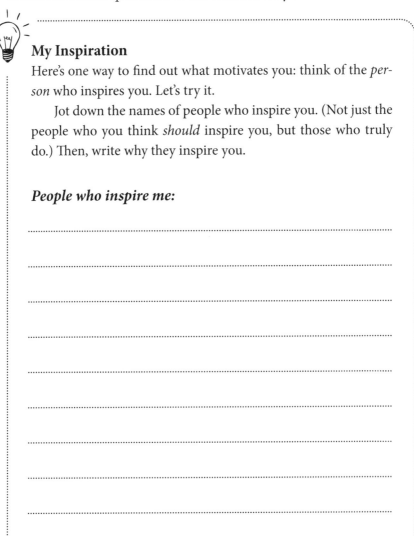

My Inspiration

Here's one way to find out what motivates you: think of the *person* who inspires you. Let's try it.

Jot down the names of people who inspire you. (Not just the people who you think *should* inspire you, but those who truly do.) Then, write why they inspire you.

People who inspire me:

Why they inspire me:

....

....

....

....

....

....

....

....

And this gets us right back to our original scenario with your friend who exclaimed, "That's so you!"

Never mind what she thinks. What do *you* think? Is your wrapping authentic? Is what you're wearing (saying, writing, doing) consistent with the things you value?

This book is about providing hints on your outside as to what's going on and who you are on the inside. It's about knowing your true contents, your value, your purpose, and your mission in a way that *shows*.

THE BIG GIG

It's what you work for all your life

So let's back up to something that just might help you understand what motivates you. When you did the exercise, did you hint at your *relationships*? Many people respond to the question of motivation by mentioning the people with whom they live or work: "I want to make a difference for the people who live here . . . I try to be a good room-mate . . . I'd do anything for my friends . . . I love my parents," etc.

True, the word "relationship" sounds touchy-feely and almost corny. But if I use the word *association*, it sounds loose and distant, and if I use the word *bond*, it's too intimate. The nice thing about the r-word is that it includes bonds and associations and every-thing in between.

A relationship is where all of this connecting, communicating, and understanding happens. So, for example, although it's brief and a bit distant, you have a relationship with the store clerk from whom you buy your shoes. You've connected and communicated in such a way that you both arrive at the understanding that she takes your money and you take the shoes. You don't really think about this unless there is a miscommunication. (You: "Oh, you mean the shoes *aren't* free?" Or, clerk: "I see that *this* money is your payment for *those* shoes.)

Obviously, other relationships run longer and deeper and have the potential for miscommunications, which may become emo-tionally charged. Your level of understanding of the communi-cations in these relationships needs to be much deeper than the understanding you have with a store clerk. And, by the way, these deeper relationships also drive you to do much of what you do (or not do) throughout your life. You often act in the quest to be under-stood, to understand others, and to find meaning for your life.

Your phone is not your friend

That cell phone sure is convenient, even life-saving at times. But your phone is not your friend. Your friend is the one sitting across the table from you or in the desk next to you or standing alongside you in line. Even the friend you don't know yet is more of a friend than your phone.

Your phone is a fabulous tool. It can assist you in your communication with others, but it must take second place to the human present to you. An authentic connection with another person can only happen *in person,* with all the "unwrapping of the gift": eye contact, body language, tone of voice, common atmosphere, shared experience, and even touch.

Try this: Next time you are seated with another person (friend or not), place your phone away and out of sight. Then, have him or her do the same. Try this for all your conversations, and you'll notice a pattern: each conversation goes longer and deeper. True, you may experience a little FOMO, but glancing at a phone while you're with someone else is *RMO* (Really Missing Out).[2]

HAPPINESS IS FRIENDSHIP

Think of your best friend. What makes her your best friend? Is it something you did? Is it something she did? Or, was it a little of what you both did, allowing the friendship to unfold (or *unwrap*)

---

[2] There's science behind this. According to Sherry Turkle, a psychologist at the Massachusetts Institute of Technology and author or *Reclaiming Conversation,* conversation is stunted and shallow even if a phone is only present and visible.

naturally as you spent time together, sharing thoughts, learning about each other, and working through the day-to-day? It is such a wonderful feeling to be understood on an intimate level that it's something we try to maintain in some way for the rest of our lives. Remember, the desire for this understanding drives—both consciously and unconsciously—much of what we do or don't do.

If we don't have a best friend, we're probably unhappy. In the very least, we feel frustrated and incomplete. In fact, a person can't be whole without relationships, especially the ones that run strong and deep. That's why one of the worst punishments for someone facing jail time is to be put into solitary confinement. It also explains why a newborn baby fails to develop emotionally—or even physically—if he isn't touched or cuddled. But even in our twenty-first-century world of epidemic loneliness, we manage to find fancier things that isolate us from our fellow human beings. For example, we love social media, photo exchanges, gaming, or texting because they can keep us in touch with friends: we watch, we share, and we laugh. But it's twisted when someone chooses to do nothing *but* digital communication and never gets out of his or her chair. We all know, after the hype has worn away, that typing letters, miles away from one another, is only a faint shadow of a real connection.

> **66** *Wishing to be friends is quick work, but friendship is a slow-ripening fruit.*
>
> — ARISTOTLE — **99**

While I was growing up, many older women told us that a woman—any woman—should not define herself by any relationship. That sounded kind of smart, and I thought that maybe these women were encouraging us to think for ourselves. (We *should* think for ourselves!) But over time, I learned that refusing to define yourself by any relationship is just as twisted as the girl who only "socializes" virtually.

Here's a strong and intelligent woman who defines herself by relationships. She began as a daughter, sister, coworker, and friend, and then later became wife to a guy named Joe and mother to me and my nine siblings. The photo on the left is from her old life as a model, and, as glamorous as this photo seems to me even today, my mom just laughs it off as having nothing to do with her real life. She always preferred to be photographed with Dad (right).

HAPPINESS IS UNDERSTANDING

Consider that feeling which comes from being understood. It's kind of nice, isn't it? Now imagine the *person* who understands you. Generally, a true friend understands you. Your best friend understands you a lot.

We know other great benefits of having a best friend, but what does it mean to *be* a friend? Your best friend can also say that you understand her because a genuine friendship does not run in only one direction.

What are the words you would use to describe a person who is a *true* friend? Let's write a list. To get you started, I've written a first quality on the lines below:

Respect,

....

....

....

....

....

Did you come up with some of your answers by thinking about friendships that lacked those qualities? For example, did you think of the word *honesty* because you know how it hurts when someone lies to you? What about this word *respect*? It might seem out of place here because respect is what you are supposed to give a parent or a boss or the police. It's not out of place at all. Respect is what you are obliged to give each and every human person no matter his or her age, religion, race, or ethnicity, but also no matter his or her level of intelligence, abilities, looks, or degree of likability. (Yes, even degree of likeability.)

And *respect* is not simply a synonym for politeness or manners, and it's certainly not just the opposite of disrespect. Respect has everything to do with acknowledging a person's *true value*. Your true purpose (or anyone's) is determined by this value.

TRUE VALUE

For centuries, people have given great value to the diamond, insisting that it's one of the most valuable things around. It's used to signify commitment (like an engagement ring), it's considered the ultimate mark of status and prestige (the "diamond club" of top performers), and access to it has been the cause of some very bloody wars.

Well, you are more valuable than all the diamonds on the Earth taken together!

In fact, you are so much more valuable, irreplaceable, and precious, that you can't even be measured on any kind of material scale. You are *in*valuable. Nothing in the world can measure your worth.

The Hope Diamond is the biggest and most famous diamond I've ever seen in person because it's right here in Washington DC at the Smithsonian Museum of Natural History. It's very large and worth anywhere between $200 and $250 million. (And yes, not even comparable to the real value of a human person!) I agree that it is quite beautiful, but the most fascinating part of its history is not very well known: apparently, its last owner, Harry Winston, donated the diamond to the Smithsonian by sending it in a box wrapped in brown paper through the U.S. Postal Service.

You know it's warped when we speak of worth only in terms of an insurance policy, a person's contribution to the economy, or the sum of a person's assets. So, you understand that it would be ridiculous to think about the amount of money your best friend is "worth" to you. Measures such as dollars, euros, or clam shells capture only the material contribution of a person.

A person is greater than the material. He or she has the potential to possess those beautiful qualities that we experience very clearly in relationships: kindness, generosity, creativity, passion, honesty, loyalty, cheerfulness, self-sacrifice, and (especially) *love*. You have the potential to possess them too. Next time someone asks you, "Hey! Do you think you are God's gift to the world?" you could correctly say, "Yes, I *know* I am."

GOD'S GIFT TO THE WORLD

Yes, that's you

There's a source to all this kindness, generosity, creativity, passion, honesty, loyalty, cheerfulness, self-sacrifice, and love. The source is God.

There comes a time in every person's life when he or she must ask certain uncomfortable and highly inconvenient questions:

Is there more to this life?

Is there anything bigger than us? Is there a someone in control?

And, why exist? Why bother to get through this cracked-up world with no hope for anything beyond it?

How could there not be anything beyond it?

These questions are preliminaries related to the earlier question about what motivates you, and all the answers have everything to do with the God who created each one of us for a purpose and an ultimate home with Him. That's why the questions are uncomfortable and inconvenient; we must put a bit of effort into finding the answers. Since ancient times, people have been anxious to get hard evidence for each answer by interpreting signs and even by demanding answers, but, as with the unwrapping of the gift of person, our personal discovery of God must also involve patient graciousness and an attitude of gratitude (much like the unwrapping in a friendship with another person). We experience the truth about God through all the beauty of this world and all the goodness of humankind, especially through relationship.[3] Even in the worst of times, beauty and goodness (and Truth) are right there, waiting to be unwrapped by our senses and rejoiced over with our whole being.[4]

Your gift of self is the greatest of these sincere gifts related to goodness (kindness, generosity, creativity, passion, honesty, loyalty, cheerfulness, self-sacrifice, and very especially love) and to beauty (God's creation and humankind's good creations).[5] God created you in his image and likeness, so it stands to reason that he'd invite you to help him share these gifts with the people around you. He personally offers additional aid so that you can grow to become the best gift you can possibly be, because you are his creation and his child, his daughter. You are his princess because he is creator and ruler of the universe.

....

[3] In the twenty-first century, we have the benefit of a record of discovery. This record is the Christian revelation and is treasured, preached, and shared by the Church and has been for about two thousand years.

[4] There's an expression that evil times produce a higher than average number of saints. In the twentieth century, war, famine, nuclear threats, and even prolonged imprisonment in gulags and concentration camps have led some to find the Truth (even amidst what is ugly and evil). People such as Victor Frankl, Corrie ten Boom, Saint Maximillian Kolbe, or Saint Teresa Benedicta of the Cross (Edith Stein) are real-life examples of people who didn't believe that when bad things happen, one can only despair.

[5] All of God's creation is good but not all of what we humans make is good.

Immaculee Ilibagiza found God through the hell that was Rwanda during the genocide of 1994. She lost her mother, father, two of her three brothers, and many of her friends and neighbors to Hutu extremists brandishing knives and machetes. She escaped the same fate by hiding in the 3' x 4' bathroom of a merciful Hutu pastor in her neighborhood. In this little bathroom, she lived with seven other people for ninety-one days! Most people under those circumstances would be tempted to dismiss the idea of a loving God and hate their enemies on the principle of "an eye for an eye," but Immaculee not only rediscovered her Catholic Faith, she forgave her persecutors and has accomplished some amazing humanitarian efforts, especially for education in her native Africa. You can read her story in her book, Left to Tell: Discovering God Amidst the Rwandan Holocaust.[6]

SUBJECT MATTERS

Experts agree that the prerequisite for successful communication is a thorough understanding of the subject matter. Even in the simplest of explanations, you've got to know your stuff. For example, when a chef writes a cookbook of all her favorite recipes, she must understand concepts such as cooking temperature, measurement, and the

---

[6] This book, *Left to Tell: Discovering God Amidst the Rwandan Holocaust* (a New York Times Bestseller), can be found on her website, www.immaculee.com, and is published by Hay House.

difference between cumin and cinnamon. (I think of the time my husband taught my son how to make pancakes by mistaking cumin for cinnamon. "Hey, they're both spices which begin with c, right?")

Are you master of your content? Do you know who you are? Let's cover four points:

You have a Dignity as a human person. (Yes, that's a capital D.) This Dignity is not dependent on how you act or dress or keep yourself clean (that's dignity with a lowercase d), but instead relates to the fact that your value is beyond material measure because you are child of God. In fact, it's beyond the value of all the mines of diamonds, or a spectacular sunrise, an extinct animal, or a solar system of planets because these things, which are wonderful and beautiful, are merely objects. You aren't an object in the way these things are objects; as a person, with an "I" or a self, you are a SUBJECT and the SUBJECT *matters* in a way an object never can. (Note that although you have a mission to be "gift," your particular gift of self is still not an "object" in the way that chocolates, flowers, or a massive diamond ring are objects.)[7]

This is also why you hear the expression, "Don't let yourself become an object." If someone views another person as an object, a "thing" to be used rather than a person to be loved, then he or she isn't acknowledging the other's true value and can justify absolutely anything such as slavery, pornography, prostitution, abuse, rape, or any number of evils.

....

[7] There's a lot written about the person "as a gift." The most prolific writer on this topic is Saint John Paul the Great who preached a body of thought called Theology of the Body.

Just imagine how the idea that each person is a SUBJECT with a unique perspective and infinite value is critical for any form of communication. You must know your own value and recognize the value of others. So, every cycle of connection, communication, and understanding must involve respect for self and respect for others.

Could you ever lose this value? If you lived like an animal long enough, could you lose any of the Dignity?

Nope. You'd have this Dignity if you were sick or homeless, in a vegetative state, or wallowing in the mud with the pigs (it just might not look very _dignified_). The exterior things such as clothing, hygiene, language, housing, or work must respect this Dignity. And as important as these exterior things are, they are only the wrapping paper I talked about earlier. No gift is ever less valuable than its wrappings.

Frederick Douglass, _a former slave and an abolitionist, is one of the most amazing heroes from our American history. He understood the worth of the human person and that slavery was not only a "crime against humanity" but an abominable sin against God. He said, "The soul that is within me no man can degrade." He also understood the gift of an education. Despite receiving no formal instruction, he learned to write powerfully and persuasively._

You have Dignity as a woman. This Dignity is equal to that of a man's, but you are different from him right down to the DNA in your cells. Your amazing female body has been designed for living in relationship, with a brain to think, mouth to speak, arms to hug, eyes to connect, ears to hear, etc. But *you also* have the added gift of being capable (by sheer design) to bear and nourish a child (who would be another human person with Dignity). This potential to help create life is more powerful than a physical ability to break a world record in weight-lifting or intellectual capacity to discover a cure for cancer.[8]

So, females are *better* than males? No, males and females are *equal* to each other, but *different* from each other. We are different, but we are complementary. We understand this from one of the most famous lines in world history: *"So God created mankind in his own image, in the image of God he created them; male and female he created them."*[9] This ancient and sacred source, a source from long before our modern thought and women's freedom movements, asserts that both men and women are created from the *same* image and are God's own.

You are a distinct individual, unique, gifted with talents to contribute to the world, and most importantly, **capable of *relationship*** and all the intangibles (related to goodness and beauty) that come along with that. As you grow, these talents and capacities mature, and, if you choose, can be put into service for the world around you, which brings us to the fact that—

....

[8]   If you read this hastily, you may come away with the idea that only females who have children have value and that is certainly not what I mean. Look again: I say "sheer design" to mean that by possessing merely the blueprints for bearing new life (even if these blueprints, the female body, are incomplete, incapable, or untasked) is the great gift. This fact, and the fact that any single life has this infinite value I described, means that even the mere (theoretical) potential to give life holds value above and beyond any object or earth-bound pursuit.

[9]   Gn. 1:27, NABRE.

You have freedom. You have the ability to make choices based upon an intellect (your mind and all its powers of reasoning) and a will (the power of your soul to desire what is good and move yourself towards that good, even against the impulses of your body). Forget what you've heard in the kind of science class that dismisses the *unseen*. You are not just a big glob of chemicals reacting to stimuli in some cosmic petri dish. Yes, you're composed of chemicals but you are more than just these chemicals. You can choose your ultimate actions, passions, thoughts, and even emotions. You have the capacity to shape yourself—with help from your Creator—into the person you aspire to be.

The real heroine

Everyone loves a good story involving "bigger than life" people who do amazing things. Women even now love stories about other women who did great things in a "man's world." Yet, there must be a great number of untold stories out there because many women were (and are) heroic in the way they have lived out their quiet lives, doing the ordinary things of each day, simply being the gift they each were designed to be.

For centuries and across every continent, Christian women have looked to Mary, the mother of Jesus Christ, as a model for many of the virtues we still cherish in the twenty-first century. While in this world, she was a Jewish woman, living in a small town. She didn't lead any armies, invent any clever things, or write any books (although according to tradition, she did tell Luke the Evangelist much of what he needed to know to write his gospel). Otherwise, she didn't say much at all! What she did, however, was cooperate with God, stay faithful through hard times, protect her child, provide for her family, pray, trust, suffer with a supernatural outlook, be a friend to those around her, and persevere to the end. None of these things are all that spectacular by themselves, but taken together as a life or a *gift*, they are greater than their sum and are beyond spectacular.

This is one of the oldest images of Mary and the child Jesus, circa 150 A.D., and is located in the Catacomb of Priscilla in Rome. (If you look closely, you can see the baby nursing at her breast.) Mary strikes a chord with people who may find life irritatingly ordinary. She's a great example of a quiet nobility even for the loudest among us . . . like me!

LOVE IS UNDERSTANDING

Understanding—*really* understanding another person because you see and respect her true value (Dignity, individuality, and freedom) and affirming her true purpose—means only one thing in the end—love.

Love between a man and woman is a special kind of mutual understanding. It's a complementary understanding (that means the opposite sexes complete each other—not compete with each other!—on many levels) and is accepting and affirming of the other person's true value and purpose.

Joe and Rosemary became my grandma and grandpa. Bet they didn't picture their son (my dad) when they were out on this date!

Enter sex right here. (Were you wondering if I'd get to it?) That complementary bit I mentioned above becomes a real physical thing in the sexual act between a man and a woman. Most women realize, long before many men do, that sex is an act of love, which involves *both* the body and the soul, and is not just another bodily function like eating. Rape wouldn't be so heinous a crime if it affected a person on only a physical level. Rape is a violation of the worst kind because it steals something that is good and beautiful by design, and because it is empty of the necessary connections, communications, understandings, and *love* that should encase, protect, and affirm sex.

Sex (the real thing) is such a powerful act of love that it's the cooperation in creating a new human life: another person in need of connection, communication, understanding, and love (which as human persons, we deserve).[10] The importance of sex is the reason that, worldwide, most of us know it must be protected by something as formal and publicly committed as marriage.

Sigmund Freud said that sex motivates most people to do just about everything they do. Sure, the human person is motivated by sexual desires, but well-adjusted people see these desires as a small part of a greater motivation to be understood in the context of love and relationship. Unfortunately, Dr. Freud didn't deal with many well-adjusted people.

Irena Sendler (1910–2008) understood the value of the human person. She was a little-known Polish woman who, during World War II, personally rescued 2,500 children from the Jewish ghetto in Warsaw from the Nazi genocide. She began as a social worker, taking care of the needs of the poor families in that neighborhood. Using her role as social worker and disguises as various utility workers, she snuck out children and infants from right under the noses of the soldiers. She was caught at one point and tortured for information on who was helping her. But she didn't give in, not even when they broke her feet and ankles.

Why did she rescue these children? They weren't related to her. The Nazis considered them as no more than garbage to be disposed of in their death camps. Irena Sendler wasn't even Jewish. Why did she allow herself to be tortured when she could have stopped the pain with a few simple words? Did she do any

[10] Sex (the real thing) should be the only thing called "sex." Anything else should not be called sex.

of this because she thought she'd be considered a hero? Was she thinking of a Nobel Peace Prize? Or was she just angry at the Nazis? She says she did it all because she understood the value of a human person—any human person. She had learned this through her Catholic faith (several faiths teach this value) and she saw her work as a simple reaction to injustice.

Irena Sendler, another woman I wish I could have known. Would you think this woman was a hero if you met her on the street?

TOTAL COMMUNICATION

Have you forgotten Fanny from earlier in this chapter? Well, don't. Her situation provides a framework for this book because communication is a lot more than words, but she hadn't figured this out.

Did her facial expressions betray thoughts she didn't intend to reveal? Was her body language sloppy and misleading? What was she wearing for the interview? What did she wear at work on a daily basis? How did she write? Had she considered her online presence or *net-iquette*?

Does she have the confidence of someone who knows her true value and purpose?

> Love is to reveal to someone: 'you are beautiful and you have value.' That is the secret of love. It's not primarily to do things for people, because then we find our glory in doing things. The secret of love is to reveal to someone that 'you are precious,' that 'you are beautiful.'
>
> — JEAN VANIER —
> *founder of L'Arche*

CHAPTER 2

Listen to Me

Listening and Speaking

Emma Woodhouse had the best intentions. She wants her friends to be happy, so she decided to set a pair of them up for a date. She imagined that they both would be fantastically happy if only they could get to know each other. Unfortunately, Emma generally talks so much that she never hears what others are saying. She managed to chatter over her friends' explanations as to why they weren't excited to be set up on a date. Although her girlfriend found the idea of a date appealing, she had some misgivings and was stressed about upcoming exams. The guy tried to excuse himself gracefully; he wasn't interested in Emma's girlfriend and, in fact, had a mild crush on Emma herself. Emma pushed things through anyway and the hapless couple ended up insulting each other at an ill-timed meeting.

All Emma had to do to avoid this situation was to stop talking so much and listen. Why not delay her project by a few weeks for the sake of her stressed girlfriend? Why couldn't she pick up the clues regarding her guy friend's true affections? Her chatter was drowning out the voices of her friends, and it called into question how much of a true friend Emma really was. But we'll give Emma the benefit of the doubt because trying to get into another person's deeper intentions is often a fruitless and silly pursuit.

WHAT DID YOU SAY?

I'm not sure I understand you.

"Listen to me!" Emma's friends say it. Emma says it. Children say it constantly. We both know you at least *think* it sometimes. I'm thinking it too, a lot (especially when people aren't listening to me at all). Every human on the planet wants to be heard because being heard is the best way to be understood. In the very least, we want some sort of attention to begin the connection that takes us there. Often, we beg for attention, maybe even do goofy things for it, unconscious of our ultimate desire for understanding.

Now look around. Everyone you know is asking for the same thing. If you want a person to listen to you, you must first listen to her so that the two of you can ultimately connect. Sure, you could stamp your feet and scream, at least getting people to look in your direction, but I don't recommend that method as a general rule—even if it works at first.

Of course, this begs the question: should getting others to listen to us be the reason why we listen to them? Well, if that were the case, we wouldn't be listening well because we'd be waiting for our chance to change the direction of any conversation. So, the answer is *no*. Besides, there are some genuine reasons to listen to other people.

When we lose ourselves in the needs of others (i.e., really listen well) not only are we better able to help them and make the world a little better because of that help, but we live according to how we were designed in the first place: as a unique and wonderful gift.

IT'S JUST TOO HARD TO DESCRIBE

You had to be there

We already know that words are powerful. But have you ever thought of the limitations of words? I'm not talking about irregular spellings or half-hearted adjectives. I'm referring to those times when you've attempted to describe a very special experience to someone only to throw your hands up in the air and exclaim, "I guess you had to be there!"

Sometimes, as I experience something cozy and joyful, rather than being lost in the moment, I think of the person who would enjoy it with me. When I first watched the sun set on the Pacific Ocean, I thought of how my husband, Robert, would take pleasure in the experience and I sighed at the thought of any future attempts to put it into language. I knew that there was just no way even the most eloquent words (or even video) could capture *exactly* the awe and power of such a beautiful experience. (And what, do you suppose, inspires a person to think of another when she is alone in a wonderful moment?)[11]

Sharing an experience, such as an everyday routine, a creative collaboration, a beautiful scene, an adventure, or even a tragedy, can bring people closer together. Words alone, no matter what

....

[11] Love!

sophisticated device you use to say them, can't equal the bonding power of shared experiences. This is why we have the sometimes frustrating tradition called "dating," which bears the responsibility of providing a couple with shared experiences. Dating (or "going out," "going steady," etc.) is good when it relies on friendship (unwrapping!) and is successful when the friendship becomes something with the potential to be a permanent, marital union.

Here's Joe and Rosemary again. Looks like they're off for another shared experience.

So, imagine the tremendous disadvantage language has without shared experiences or, in the very least, without personal contact. Face-to-face communication adds an extra layer of facial expressions, gestures, and context, which can help us understand more fully what the other person is trying to communicate. Think about all the times you've received a text that should have been a phone call, or a phone call that should have been a visit in person. The more we are removed from shared experience or face-to-face interaction, the more remote and garbled a communication can become.

Flip this idea around. If you know you haven't conveyed the feel or the awe of an experience, imagine how little you've picked up on another person's attempts to convey her feelings, ideas, and experiences. It makes you wonder about all those digital bits she's sent you, doesn't it?

How to date
Without losing your mind

Dating is a tradition that is rather recent in human history. In the old days, marriages were simply arranged by the parents or local community, and in those few places where they weren't, the idea of *courting* or some other sort of prescribed ritual provided a framework for how the sexes interacted while unmarried and "available."

Dating might be frustrating, but my parents did it. My grandparents did it too. Well, I'm here, aren't I? Dating can be a little less frustrating when all parties involved follow some simple ground rules. In this, women can lead the way:

1. Dating is not just the thing we do with the guy who serves as our "significant other" for a certain, unpredictable period of time. Dating is *ultimately* about finding your lifelong soul mate, your husband, but it's okay to go out on casual, friendly dates with different guys, developing friendships and getting to know each one a bit better. But you must be clear with them as to the nature and limits of the friendship. Gradually you will realize that there is one with whom you "click" better than the others; hopefully he will feel the same way!

2. A dinner, a movie, or a whole bunch of dates don't mean that you are obliged to pay back with anything. You don't owe a guy money or a kiss or anything else.

3. Don't mislead a guy into thinking that you are interested in a mutually exclusive relationship with him. If you aren't interested in him, do not continue seeing him in one-on-one prearranged situations (i.e., dates).

4. Let the fellow do the asking for a date. Give him a chance. If it's painful to watch him try, help him along, but let him build a little confidence by asking, planning, and, if appropriate, picking you up from your home.

5. Let him pay for the date when he offers. If you continue dating someone who is obviously stretching beyond his financial means and you are interested in spending time with him, encourage free venues like a walk or a visit to a park.

6. Let him open the door for you if he tries. For that matter, let anyone open the door for you. Many men have been bullied into not opening doors by women who are determined to be treated like men. Let him know with your body language that it's okay. (Don't gush "thank you!" every time he does it though. A smile is enough.)

7. Be authentic while you're with a guy. Don't attempt to have him worship you as some sort of goddess or humble him by showing off how tough you are. Be yourself and foster a friendship with him. Some dates lead only to friendship, but a new friend is a treasure. Besides, remember that a marriage must be based on friendship.

8. On the other hand, mind your manners. Being authentic doesn't mean babbling on or stuffing your face like it's your last meal. Use all the guidelines for communication and etiquette presented in these chapters.

9. Don't overwhelm him with a discussion of your feelings, a list of past personal injuries, old boyfriends, or negativity in general. The poor dude just asked you out on a date, not a therapy session.

10. Finally, don't be anxious. Don't be anxious about him, the date, having a boyfriend, or getting married. Be calm, cool, and collected. Be a lady and expect to be treated as a lady.

So now you're saying, *"Whoa! I'm not ready for marriage!"* And so, you're not. Go out in groups of friends instead. You can learn a lot about men from the way they interact under those conditions.

CONNECTIONS

An authentic relationship can't get started without a connection, an *in-person* connection. Often, you first connect with someone else in a group setting, and in a group setting, many other things like personalities, features of the language, and even noisy surroundings can affect how well you are able to connect with others.

Think of all the times you are called upon to connect with others, perhaps for the first time: parties, shopping, family gatherings, school, clubs, jobs, sports, or just hanging around with friends. You can see how each of your friends has a personality that comes out as early as a handshake or greeting. Sometimes you watch a newcomer to see how he reacts to your friends, and you might wonder what's crossing his mind.

Now imagine what connection style others pick up from *you*. Let's consider the way in which you connect with others (choose your best answer for each connection scenario):

1. When I walk into a room filled with people I don't know, I . . .

a. *wave and say hello to as many people as I can. I glance around a lot, perhaps looking for the fun or the opportunity to have fun. I'm open to new people and I easily smile when I greet newcomers.*

b. *look for the people who may hold opportunity for me. If no one looks promising, I'll lose myself in my phone, perhaps checking to see if something better is happening someplace else.*

c. *see who comes my way and try to engage her in real conversation rather than meaningless chatter. I'm hoping I can make it through the chore of small talk, and I think it's just fine if I don't meet anyone new.*

d. *find my friends and try to initiate conversations that make everyone feel comfortable, even if I have to downplay what I really want to talk about. I'm open to meeting new people, especially if they could become good friends, but old friends come first.*

2. When listening to an acquaintance say something about herself which bothers me, I . . .

a. *will either change the subject by speaking of something happier or even more exciting, or I will point out how what she said isn't really as bad as she thinks. I might even think that there's an upside to what she's said.*

b. will correct her and set her straight.

c. wonder about the person and then wonder who else bothers me. I will worry about the fact that maybe I do the same bothersome thing. I will formulate some ways of responding to her, but will remain silent as I reject each formulation. I begin to think maybe I should have stayed home.

d. will sit uncomfortably but will let her speak. I won't say anything.

3. When someone shares good news about herself, I . . .

a. enthusiastically congratulate her and tell a similar story about myself in similar circumstances. Or maybe I tell an even better story about myself.

b. briefly acknowledge the news and steer the conversation away from her news to matters immediately at hand (or my own news).

c. wonder when her luck will change, probe for some detail, and perhaps provide a cautionary tale of how she should watch out for a change in luck. And, if she is a very good friend, I will remember to congratulate her.

d. smile, congratulate, and monitor my reaction to reinforce the speaker's good feelings.

4. When I must break bad news to someone, I . . .

a. consider it critical to see her in person. Sometimes though (because I have procrastinated in meeting with her for so long) I will call her or ask her to give me a call. I may craft an email, but likely will not send it.

b. *tell her the next chance I get even if it's unfortunately a text. I know I just can't be overly concerned about feelings in this situation.*

c. *carefully plan the best way to break the news and write an email. A long letter or email would be a backup plan. Sometimes I generalize the bad news to newer (imaginary) situations. If I wait too long to pass along the bad news, and run into the person, I am likely to blurt it out in a less than ideal way. (NOTE: melancholics don't usually realize this about themselves. They can be very blunt and give bad news in the worst possible way, without realizing it. Usually they HATE to do this in person, unless they are partly choleric.)*

d. *can't stand the thought of making her so unhappy, but I attempt to do it in the briefest, least painful way, sometimes at the risk of not being clear.*

5. **When asked to provide background about myself or share some experiences, I . . .**

a. *spontaneously craft a fun version of myself with quite a bit of embellishing. (I'm used to doing this sort of thing.)*

b. *give the facts of what I've done, especially my many important achievements.*

c. *get kind of philosophical about my background and hope that the listener is with me on it.*

d. *tell things about myself truthfully but with careful attention to what I think the listener wants to hear.*

a. _____   b. _____   c. _____   d. _____

Now tally up your a's, b's, c's and d's. You probably have a mix, but you can still detect a pattern. See if any of the following rings true.

If you answered mostly **A**, your temperament is most likely sanguine. You are optimistic and generally pleasant. You can excite others around you and get them to see the big picture, but you may fall short on the details and leave things unfinished. You could be called **"Miss Sunshine"** (but who needs labels?)

If you answered mostly **B**, your temperament is most likely choleric. You are assertive and direct. You get things done and can stay very focused even when others aren't. You may have heard your name and the term **"Bossy Pants"** in the same sentence. (But of course that's not going to bother you if it gets stuff done.)

If you answered mostly **C**, your temperament is most likely melancholic. You are thoughtful and deep. Sometimes you get discouraged and at your worst, pessimistic, but you are self-aware and are able to distinguish the good from the bad. Just don't let them call you the **"Rain on the Parade."**

If you answered mostly **D**, your temperament is most likely phlegmatic. You are reliable, loyal, and overall quite pleasant. You are the peacemaker in your crowd; however, sometimes you can get pushed around or crowded out so that your voice isn't heard when it needs to be. If you had to choose a nickname, it might be the **"Get-Along Gal."** (But remember, it's okay not to be labeled.)

This connection and communication stuff is as old as the ancient Greeks.[12] It's not about fanciful (and false) astrology or even mere brain chemistry. It's about a set of reactions that come naturally to you. But return to my discussion on "Subject Matters" and recall that you have free will. You have the ability to choose to react in a certain way. You can shape yourself into the person you want to be.

Rules for everyone to follow regardless of your personal connection style:

Generally, connections should be about listening first:

1. Greet a new person as if she might one day become a friend. Smile and learn her name. Say it back to her: for example, "Nice to meet you, Jane."

2. You are taking in a lot of sensory information when you meet a new person, but resist the temptation to judge her, even if only in your head. (We'll get to judging books by their covers in the next chapter.) Listen to what is said and assume there is more to a story if something seems amiss or a bit mysterious. She is not obligated to tell you the background story to everything she's saying.

3. Pay attention to a speaker with your whole face. Look at her in the eyes and give her feedback with questions, rather than saying *uh huh* or one-upping with your own stories and opinions.

....

[12] For more on this topic, read *The Temperament God Gave You* by Art and Laraine Bennett. It is one of the most useful books you'll ever read!

(Be conscious of this: most people one-up more than they think they do.)

4. Just because something is on your mind, doesn't mean you must give words to it. Believe it or not, the person may find the information boring, embarrassing, or irrelevant.

5. When the time is right, provide information about yourself. Never, under any circumstances, provide comparisons between yourself and other people (present or not) that demeans yourself (or even looks like that) or sounds like gossip.

6. Identify the things about your communication style that need improvement. Consciously monitor yourself in situations where you need the improvement. Later, reflect upon how well you connected with the person or people.

> 66 *Any fool can criticize, condemn, and complain and most fools do.*
>
> — BEN FRANKLIN —
> *(a Mr. Sunshine, if you will)* 99

Maybe the phrase "Rain on the parade" is a little negative and needs to be revisited for a bit of clarification. The philosopher, Edith Stein, now called Saint Theresa of the Cross for her heroic life and death in a Nazi concentration camp, once provided a good description for how some qualities of the melancholic should be a guide for every woman. *"The soul of woman must be expansive and open to all human beings, it must be quiet so that no small weak flame will be extinguished by storm winds; warm so as not to benumb fragile buds . . . empty of itself, in order that extraneous life may have room in it; finally mistress of itself and also of its body, so that the entire person is readily at the disposal of every call."*[13]

I was fortunate as a college student to have discovered the writings of Edith Stein. She was a Jewish intellectual who contributed to a school of philosophy called Phenomenology. Later, she fine-tuned her thinking in the light of her own conversion to the Christian Faith and wrote extensively on the vocation of women.

[13] It's been speculated that Edith had a melancholic temperament and I thank God for that because maybe she wouldn't have had the inclination to sit down and write all the wonderful things she's written.

Let's shake on it!

In the United States, we shake hands when we meet new people. In the old days, a woman's hand was kissed by a man, and in other cultures, cheeks might be kissed. In most of Asia, people bow to one another.

Even as our world shrinks and becomes more multicultural, you will now, more than ever, be shaking hands in both the professional and social worlds. Here's how you give a great handshake:

1. Extend your right hand in the direction and at the level of the other's right hand. Your thumb should be pointing up.

2. Grasp his hand firmly but not tightly (like your grip on a door knob while opening a door). Most importantly, don't give him the "dead fish" (i.e., a floppy hand).

3. Look him in the eyes. Smile confidently.

4. Say, "Nice to meet you, Mr. Knightley," Or, "Hi, Frederick!"

5. Americans usually pump about three times. You can loosen after that and place your hand back to your side.

6. My advice is that you learn how *not* to think about it. Develop the habit of a good handshake and use your mental energy on your new friend.

Exceptions:

*   If someone extends his left hand, there is a reason (perhaps medical). Extend your left hand and shake.
*   If someone refuses to extend his hand, don't force the issue, and don't take it as a personal insult. (His reasons might be very good.)
*   If you are in a place where handshaking is not the dominant greeting, learn the local custom.

WHAT'S A BODY TO SAY?

It's already blabbing on about something.

Have you ever watched a conversation where one of the speakers never gave any visual clues to what she was saying or speaking? It's quite striking, isn't it? She doesn't smile or nod or shake her head. She doesn't move her eyebrows or shoulders. She is, as the saying goes, *hard to read.*

That's a very appropriate expression. When we communicate with any other soul, we not only listen to words, intonations, and pitch, we also pick up on visual cues. We infer meaning from all the physical signals a speaker sends, both conscious and unconscious.

A classic example is the inference many people will make, whether accurate or not, that a person is feeling the need for extra security because her arms are folded in front of her body as if she is trying to place a barrier between herself and the rest of the world. Then, there is the cue that someone isn't paying attention to what you are saying because she won't turn her face to meet yours, or ever once glance into your eyes.

Body language consists of physical positions, gestures, facial expressions, and micro-facial expressions. In the interest of fostering clear and concise communications, below is a guide to using body language that shows you are open and attentive.

1. Stand up straight. Ensure that your shoulders are back and your chin is raised (*not* tilted) when facing others.

2. Maintain eye contact while conversing with someone. If you are speaking to a group of people, establish eye contact with each

person in a natural and graceful rotation. Be conscious of not leaving any one person out of your loop of eye contact.

3. When smiling is appropriate, smile with your eyes as well as your mouth.

4. If you are sitting as you speak to others, sit up straight with your knees together. If you are in a very casual setting, you may cross your legs, but don't tighten up into a coil or splay your thighs apart. Point your toes in the direction of the person to whom you are speaking.

5. Resist folding your arms while either sitting or standing. Rather, use your hands to gesture gently, keeping them away from your face and hair, avoiding things like air quotes, pointing toward people, or twirling your jewelry.

What's in a name?

When I was in grade school the boys had this annoying habit of referring to the girls by only their last names. So, a conversation went like this:

Boy: Hey You! Girl with the dorky pig tails!
Me in first grade: Me? Uh, the name is Mary.
Boy: Use your feet for kickball, not your hands.

Boy: Sheehan!
Me in eighth grade: What?
Boy: Use your feet for kickball, not your hands.

Later, in high school when the boys used our first names, I can remember the distinct pleasure of the sound of my name from someone other than a teacher or girl. In fact, to this day, in a reflective moment, I feel that warm tingle of connection when my husband addresses me by my first name.

A name is a mighty thing! It is the one word floating through space that identifies me—myself (body and soul): not my sister, not my friend, not my mother, not my daughter—me. When my name is mispronounced (accidentally or otherwise) it's a bit of a punch to the stomach because it seems more than a simple jumble of sounds and more like a misunderstanding.

How did first names get started? Experts (people who study *anthroponomastics)* agree that every name was once a word, a word like "toothless" or "blonde" or "gentle." So, for example, the name "Calvin" is "bald" in Latin. The same experts suspect that humans have been applying words to people for so long that we have no record of a culture referring to any person as "girl number 5462" or "Old Man G-532."

Of course, this meaning behind a name means one must be very careful when choosing a child's name. After all, the poor kid will have to either live up to it or live it down.

Some examples:

Amanda, Amy—*amare,* "to love" (Latin)

Averil—*hild,* "fight" (Old English)

Clare, Clara, Claire, Clarissa—*clarus,* "bright, clear" (French/Latin)

Emily, Amelia—*oaemulus,* "rivaling" (Latin)

Fatima—*fatimah,* "baby's nurse; woman who breast feeds" (Arabic)

Grace, Gracie—*gratia*, "grace" (Latin)

Mira—*meri*, "great, famous" (Slavonic)

Sophia—*sofia*, "wisdom" (Greek)

That's a pretty incomplete list. Experts say that the variety of names today is so large that each individual name is loaded with more meaning than ever before.[14]

> "
> Regard your good name as the richest jewel you can possibly be possessed of——for credit is like fire; when once you have kindled it you may easily preserve it, but if you once extinguish it, you will find it an arduous task to rekindle it again. The way to gain a good reputation is to endeavor what you desire to appear.
>
> — SOCRATES —
>
> *ancient Greek philosopher and well-rounded guy*
> "

---

[14] An expert named Laura Wattenberg has written extensively on the evolution of naming babies.

MISS SUNSHINE LEARNS THE HARD WAY

But she's not discouraged at all

Yes, Emma above has a sanguine temperament. She's also slightly bossy, if truth be told. Okay. Now what?

Well, she can certainly learn to make the most of her best connection traits and overcome the, shall we say, obnoxious ones.

If Emma reflects upon what went wrong in her interactions with her friends, she'll realize that all her assumptions about her friends were inaccurate because she never really connected with them. The attention wasn't there because she didn't listen. A lack of true connection often happens when we first meet people, but it can happen even after we've become friends.

Even if you aren't a *Miss Sunshine*, there are still ways you can improve your connection style. For each connection style there are related strengths and weaknesses involved in any relationship. Let's look at each in terms of what makes a person a great friend: being enjoyable company, truthfulness, reliability, and, very importantly, respect.

	BEING ENJOYABLE COMPANY	TRUTHFULNESS	RELIABILITY	RESPECT
MISS SUNSHINE	Continue your cheerfulness and your genuine laughter, but listen to others and allow them to take center stage sometimes.	Stick to the truth even if it's boring. On the other hand, don't give it all away all the time (TMI!). Keep some things private.	You've got the best intentions, but follow through with what you've started and meet deadlines.	Be courteous of a person's time by showing up when you said you would. Give a person plenty of time to speak when it's her turn.
BOSSY PANTS	Smile even when it's hard, and greet people cheerfully. Laugh to be enjoyable company, not when something ironic happens or someone looks foolish.	Continue being truthful but monitor how and when you should do so. Be sensitive.	You might be very reliable, but be forgiving with others who may struggle with it.	Say *thank you* when people do something for you rather than assuming it should have been done anyway. Avoid finishing people's sentences and generally respect their freedom.
RAIN ON THE PARADE	Get out and be around people. Smile and greet people cheerfully, even when it's difficult to do so. Find the bright side of a situation more often.	Consider first what needs to be told. Yes, be truthful, but sometimes it's not necessary to convey all the bleak details.	Strive to be a team player.	Respect the rights of others to have opinions other than your own. Always listen to another's point of view even if it doesn't seem very reasonable to you.
GET-ALONG GAL	Continue to smile and accommodate when appropriate, but suggest things to do even if you think your opinion may not be a big hit with everyone.	Tell the truth even if it might offend someone. Use your people skills to break bad news.	Continue to be reliable, but hold accountable those who refuse to come through for you.	Continue to listen well and be tolerant of others. Be assertive when justice calls for it.

Jane Austen had such a keen eye and a wise soul: "But a sanguine temper, forever expecting more good than occurs, does not always pay for its hopes by any proportion of depression. It soon flies over the present failure and begins to hope again." We should have asked Jane Austen about psychology and the value of relationships rather than Sigmund Freud. Well, it's not too late to learn.

CONNECTING AGAIN AND AGAIN

. . . and it's called friendship

You can see how communicating to understand and to be understood is about connecting—and connecting again. While you'd think it might get easier with repeated conversations or experiences, it often doesn't (even though it certainly can when you allow it).

For example, I make the effort to be a great listener and attentive partner whenever I meet someone new, but my own children complain that I zone out sometimes when they attempt to capture my attention. I guess you could say I'm refusing to connect. (And to think I wrote a book on this!) The reason may be no excuse at all, but once my attention is activated, these same children must admit that I do give them my all. (I really do!)

One could argue that with familiar people, it's perfectly appropriate to be comfortable or casual, so that perhaps what appears to be a lack of attention or concern is really just an ability to multitask with the extra energy left over from not having to get to know the speaker in the first place. To test this theory, all one would have to do is check the understanding of the listener because, generally, a connection is not made without listening, and multitasking is really a fancy way to say "distracted." (That's not just my theory. The brain experts have claimed this is true.)[15]

So, giving your full attention and sincere effort in your connections with your roommate, your sister, a coworker, or a parent is at least as important as when you meet someone new, interview for a job, or concentrate in a class at school. The so-called "left over" energy we think is available from not having to concentrate on new names, first impressions, or extra details really isn't ever left to use because it's tapped to fuel other things, like comprehending familiar information in a new context or new information in a familiar context, or creating a deeper understanding of the other person. In the case of my children, it's a good thing they know their mother well enough to see that I'm not dismissing their concerns; I'm just old and tired (not an excuse, I know). Indeed, I'm not so sure anyone besides my children would be so understanding. (God bless them!) Mutual understanding and attention from both parties is essential for good communication.

....

[15] That reminds me of another good book called *Your Brain at Work: Strategies for Overcoming Distraction, Regaining Focus, and Working Smarter All Day Long* by David Rock (Harper Collins, 2009).

Reactions
or how not to go nuclear

What if you're listening well, but you don't like what you hear and you are ready to lose your temper? Or, maybe you have been listening beautifully, but find you've become stuck on something disturbing. In fact, you feel insulted. Maybe hurt. Are you listening anymore?

Probably not. Communication experts claim that if we think through our communications (sort of communicate to ourselves about a communication at hand) we will be better able to reappraise and react appropriately and justly. *Appropriate* and *just* translate into *gracious* and *fair*.

So, for example,

Mr. Collins says: "Your brownies are nothing like Mrs. D's!"

You think (and you're about ready to say): "You nasty %*&#! So you think I'm not as good as Mrs. D?"

This is when you STOP. Then, take a breath and recognize your own feelings toward the statement, controlling your urge to respond. (Yes, this can all take place in a split second if you breathe.) Think through an inner conversation like below:

I feel offended by this statement, but is it a truly offensive statement? (Reappraise.)

Maybe. I don't know if he's trying to offend. I'll give him the benefit of the doubt. Okay, move on.

Or, no. He's not being offensive. That's silly. Why would it matter anyway? (It doesn't.) Okay, move on.

Or, finally, yes. The evidence suggests he's trying to offend me. So my choices are:

1. Ignore the statement. After all, does it really matter?

2. Defend myself and my brownies.

3. Say something nasty about him or Mrs. D. or Mrs. D.'s brownies.

In the case of someone's clear insult, (which doesn't happen as often as you might think) number 3 is out because saying something nasty will not make me feel better. (Well, maybe for a fleeting ten seconds, but not in the long run.) It will also not change Mr. Collin's opinion on the brownie issue. And who is Mrs. D anyway?

Number 2 is probably a huge waste of energy because (maybe) I'm really not that passionate about my brownies anyway.

Even if I were passionate about brownie-making, no insult can ever reduce the value of my brownie-making.

Okay, Number 1. *You say:* "Oh Mr. Collins, would you like some coffee with the brownies?"[16]

---

[16] In some, more serious discussions, not only will you be called not to go nuclear on the other person, but you need to correct the record. Learning informal logic will help with this, so that any statement you make or reply you give is logical and, therefore, effective. (In other words, you don't want to simply throw out insults, generalize inappropriately, or dodge the core issues.) The book, *The Fallacy Detective*, by Nathaniel and Hans Bluedorn, provides an easy way to train yourself.

WITH GREAT POWER

comes great responsibility

One of the greatest powers you have as a human person is your ability for spoken language. Sure, birds sing, whales click and whistle, and my old dog Bruno could tell me all sorts of things with just his sweet doggie eyes.

But *you*! You can create and group sounds in such a way that I can know that you had a delicious mocha-almond ice cream for dessert last night, that you have a little brother who gives you grief, and that you want to one day be the Ambassador to Thailand because of your passion to assist developing nations, your interest in South Asian culture, and your talent for language. Those are complex notions that Bruno can't transmit, much less actually have.

Sojournor Truth was an uneducated slave from New York, who only spoke Dutch until she was nine, when she was sold away from her family along with a flock of sheep. Later she would escape slavery with one of her babies and become one of the greatest influences on sex and racial equality. She learned (in a new language, I might add) how to connect with her listeners and inspire others to change.

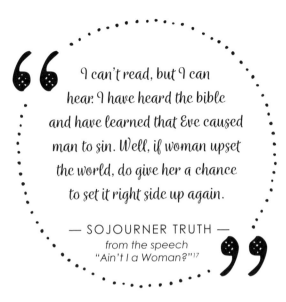

I can't read, but I can hear. I have heard the bible and have learned that Eve caused man to sin. Well, if woman upset the world, do give her a chance to set it right side up again.

— SOJOURNER TRUTH —
from the speech "Ain't I a Woman?"[17]

But we take this power for granted. In the day-to-day business of talking with our friends, there are a few simple rules for clear and cognizant communication. From there we can let our imagination flourish. Let's get to them with a question:

....

17 Sojourner Truth didn't write out "Aint I a Woman?" It was recorded after she gave the speech. This quote is from the records of Marius Robinson (Anti-Slavery Bugle, June 21, 1851). Another reporter said she walked up to speak "like a queen."

WHAT DO A GUN, A DIAPER, AND SANTA'S SLEIGH HAVE IN COMMON?

They're loaded. Like words.

Words can destroy, demoralize, disgust, or delight.

Think of what comes out of a **gun**. Language that works like it:

- demeaning terms

- labels (sometimes even seemingly neutral ones, because these can hold unreasonable demands or be grossly off target)

- racist or bigoted comments or labels

- judgments (of a person)[18]

- gossip

- lies

Think of what's in a **diaper**. Yeah, *that*. Language that works like it:

- cuss words and oaths

- crudeness and vulgarity (TMI, *too much information*)

- obscenity

....

[18] Here's a chance to clarify the difference between judging a person and judging an action. You should never judge a person, but you have an intellect that judges *actions* all the time. You know if something is right or wrong and you call it as you see it. Telling someone that an action is right or wrong is not judging a person.

Think of what's loaded up into **Santa's sleigh**. Gifts! Language that works like it:

- sincere affirmation

- genuine humor

- constructive advice

- inspiration

- a person's preferred name

- "I love you!"

So, before you are tempted to trash talk the girl in the desk next to you, ask yourself, "Are the words I'm getting ready to say loaded like a gun, a diaper, or Santa's sleigh?" And, once determined, remember these **three rules:**

- **Firing a gun can kill or hurt someone.** *Don't do it.*

- **A diaper is filled with nastiness.** *Change it.*

- **Santa's Sleigh brings wonderful things that work magic in people's hearts.** *Bring on the magic!*

BRING IT ON

and watch the magic!

How do you package your magic? (Another way is to ask how you "wrap your gift?") Do you speak in a way that's appealing? Can you hold the attention of your listener in the conversations of daily life? Monitor yourself using these suggestions:

1. Always listen to your conversation partner. Think through any response you may feel inspired to give, but don't take for granted his or her desire for a response.

2. Breathe while you speak. Speak at a comfortable and natural pitch. Adjust your volume so that only your conversation partner can hear you, especially in a public place like a restaurant or shop. (You know what "loud talkers" sound like and it's not pretty.)

3. Avoid making statements as if they are questions: "I'm an accountant?" Say instead, "I'm an accountant" (intonate *downward* in pitch on the last syllable).

4. Maintain eye contact without freaking out your conversation partner. (That means looking away naturally now and then.) Nod your head when appropriate.

5. Rid your speaking of unhealthy fillers, such as "like," "um," "uh," "huh," or "hmm." Anything that is not a word is generally best left unsaid.

6. Avoid extremes in pace. Speak in a way you'd like others to speak, neither too quickly nor too slowly.

7. Monitor the attention of your listeners through their body language and eye movements. If you've directed the conversation toward yourself, resorted to negativity or gossip, or wandered off topic, you may have lost them already.

A laughing matter

We've always associated laughter with some of the best things in life: happiness, humor, and friendship. Now we know that laughter is also about bonding and trust, and is even good for our health because it strengthens the immune system, reduces pain, and improves lung capacity (among other things). These benefits partly explain why there are whole businesses built around the production of laughter, like stand-up comedy, sitcoms, movies, musicals, and even *laugh* yoga.

Laughing is an automatic, physical response of the body to the mind's comprehension of an incongruence (absurdity, irony, surprise, etc.) and involves many parts of the brain, as we must listen and/or see, process the stimulation, comprehend and interpret, "get" it, and then signal the rest of the body to react with shortened breaths, gasps, mouth movements, and maybe even belly-clutching if it's a good joke, surprise, whatever.

Biologists say that laughter is a primitive reaction we possess from the days when we might outrun a saber-tooth tiger or outsmart a poisonous snake.

Caveman #1: Wow, that was close! We were almost eaten alive!

Caveman #2: You should have seen your face when that tiger bared its teeth. Ha!

Caveman #1: Ha ha ha ha ha! You looked funny too! Ha ha ha ha ha!

Apparently, that sudden relief after so much stress allows the body to put its guard down, recover, and relax the "flight or fight" instinct. Once genuine laughter has started, it signals trust to those around you. (You might laugh at your fellow cave person, but not in the face of the saber-tooth tiger.)

When we transmit this trust (let our guard down), we connect with others and strengthen any bond. Indeed, one reason why sarcasm used in a passive-aggressive way is so naturally unlikable is because the laughter (and supposed humor) that comes with it betrays the real purpose of laughter. There is no connection or bonding, only *dis*connection and possibly hurt.

Another awful way that laughter betrays its real purpose is when a group laughs at an individual rather than *with* the individual. Everyone is putting his or her guard down and de-stressing at the expense of someone's sense of self-worth. Usually, such laughter comes easily for people who feel they need a boost for their own egos or a cover for what they feel is lacking in themselves.

FROG AND TOAD ARE FRIENDS

How many books and gurus have advised you not to gossip, lie, or use sarcasm? (Lots!) But we both know it's all more easily said than done. Many of these people who advise against such negative language talk very little about the *struggle* against gossiping, lying, or being a sarcastic jerk.

A struggle is the internal fight a person keeps up to improve her behavior so that it conforms to the standard she chooses by her intellect. Believe it or not, the struggle we make to be better *actually makes us better.* We rise closer to the standard we've set for ourselves with each sincere attempt.

A struggle is enabled by free will and is moved along by will-power. Remember, when you were little and you read the part in *Frog and Toad Together* about willpower and cookies?[19]

"We must stop eating!" cried Toad as he ate another [cookie].

"Yes," said Frog, reaching for another cookie, "we need will power."

"What is will power?" asked Toad.

"Will power is trying hard not to do something that you really want to do," said Frog.

"You mean like trying not to eat all of these cookies?" asked Toad.

"Right," said Frog.

An image of poor Toad and his cookie jar is a great way to remember this idea of willpower, but try to forget the sad ending when he finally throws the cookies to the birds, complaining that he's disgusted with the whole thing, and goes home to bake a cake. (Sorry if I spoiled the ending for you.)

Thankfully, toads are not only *not* human, but they aren't particularly known for their virtue either. (Actually, only we humans can be virtuous; animals operate only on instinct and brain chemistry.)

....

[19] If you haven't read *Frog and Toad Together* by Arnold Lobel, read it soon. And, if you have read it, you may have noted that Toad is a bit of a *Rain on the Parade* and Frog is a *Mr. Sunshine.*

A virtue is a conscious habit or a regular way of behaving, which can be strengthened over time so that it helps a person win the struggle to be good. (That's *good* as in all things in keeping with the truth about your worth and purpose.)

After all, you can't communicate good things like honesty, justice, or self-control unless you actually *are* honest, just, and self-controlled.[20]

A BEAUTIFUL TABLE

with four sturdy legs

I bet you've heard the expression, "Don't just tell me; show me." It's not only a statement about good teaching technique, it's a plea for authenticity in our communication. No one likes insincerity or hypocrisy, and our best way to communicate about ourselves is through our own example, our actions.

Who am I? I want to answer that question with my whole self, with both my words and my actions.

Of course, I'm a work in progress. But I can work toward a four-leg foundation (like a table) of good communication. If any one leg is missing, the table is unstable or even shaky (and from my table would fall a laptop, pile of papers, cup of hot coffee, and whatever bit of food I happen to have at the moment). In communication, if any one of the legs below is missing, the table is wobbly—my communication is insincere, hypocritical, or, at worst, fraudulent. (So, things will fall. People will get hurt.)

....

20   See Chapter 6 for a comprehensive list of the virtues.

First Leg: Justice in my communication	Second Leg: Good judgment in my communication
• I'm fair to others in what I say; I withhold judgment of people. • I withhold information that could hurt the reputation of someone. • I provide the information needed to help someone.	• I speak to the person who needs to hear what I have to say. I avoid having others overhear what I say if they don't need to hear it. • I choose the right time to speak. • I avoid speaking when I am angry or frustrated. I wait to cool off.
Third Leg: *Self-control in my communication*	**Fourth Leg:** *Persistence in my communication*
• I resist the temptation to exaggerate or lie. • I allow others to speak even when I have a lot to say. • I stop speaking when I've made my point.	• I tell the truth even if it's not popular. • I follow up with people who need to have the information I'm sharing. I do not nag, however. • I check for understanding of what I've shared.

The virtues of public speaking
(or, how to do it)

Consider all the virtues you must put into action while communicating in front of a group. There's prudence and/or justice in the choice of topics, industriousness in the preparation, courage in standing there in the first place, fortitude in staying in front of everyone, self-discipline in sticking to your speech or talk, patience in reading and listening to your audience, and humility in not getting a big head when you've done one FABULOUS job!

Toastmasters International, an organization that teaches people the art of public speaking, advises some of the following tips for becoming a world-class speaker:

1. Know your topic. Master the subject matter. Read the background information of what you are covering so that you are able to answer questions. Learn to love the topic, or at least to love the challenge of speaking on it.

2. Know your audience. You can introduce yourself to people as they come into the venue before you begin to speak, to help reduce the anxiety of speaking to strangers.

3. Practice your talk or speech with all the equipment you plan to use.

4. Know the venue. Check over the room, the seating arrangement, and look at the podium. Stand at the podium and look out to an imaginary audience.

5. Visualize yourself giving the speech and giving it well. Visualize a happy audience, clapping at the end.

6. As you come up to speak, know that a little nervous energy is a good thing. It will put you on your game and help you to think on your feet. Relax, take a deep breath, and count to five before you begin speaking.

7. Do not say, "Sorry, I'm a little nervous," or, "Whoops, I made a mistake." Just slow down, breathe, and continue on.

8. Remember, the audience wants you to succeed. Ride on that energy.[21]

9. Concentrate on the content of your speech, not on yourself.

10. Take every opportunity to speak publicly and gain experience.

---

[21] This tip seems counterintuitive, but consider your feelings when you're in an audience. You really want the speaker to do well, don't you? You may not know why, but the feeling is there. This tip comes specifically from the Toastmasters International website which has an amazing amount of helpful information. See www.toastmasters.org.

Helen Keller

You probably know the story of Helen Keller, the woman who lost her hearing and her sight as a baby. But few of us will ever experience the incredible horror of being *completely unable to connect with others* through conventional language. One reason why her teacher, Annie Sullivan, was such a miracle worker is because she managed to give the gift of language to Helen so that she could one day connect, communicate, and understand: in short, to have meaningful relationships (i.e., express love). This made the difference between Helen remaining on the level of an uncontrollable "problem for people to solve" to a world-class problem solver herself.

"I long to accomplish a great and noble task, but it is my chief duty to accomplish humble tasks as though they were great and noble. The world is moved along, not only by the mighty shoves of its heroes, but also by the aggregate of the tiny pushes of each honest worker."[22]

---

[22] For the full story, read the play, *The Miracle Worker*, by William Gibson.

CHAPTER 3

Look at That

The Possibilities of Fashion

What if I told you that the guy below will one day be your husband:

What are you thinking now?[23]

---

[23] But he's a great guy! (No, he is not my husband.)

The connections we make with other people often don't start with words, but with visual first impressions, which generally get a head start on words by seconds, minutes, or much longer. Then, words and gestures may have to struggle with that impression to counteract any negative feelings. Or, maybe they aren't called to that struggle because everything has gone along swimmingly. (Phew!) Most often it takes a very long time for a person's words and actions to overturn a first impression, but when it finally happens, it might be too late to change someone's mind.

IS THIS GUY FOR REAL?

and does he go out in public like that?

Well, that's the power of a first impression! You've been wired to take in the world through your senses, make some general assumptions, and then determine action from there.

If we break down the first impression above, we can see that our assumptions aren't so much about the person himself, but the person's *choice* for footwear . . . and hosiery, and those cargo shorts! We instinctively assume that the choice for what one wears is a sort of value judgment on his or her part. That's certainly true, but to go deeper, we must investigate what clothing really is.

Fashion historians (and other experts concerned with the human condition) agree that there are two purposes to clothing: 1. protection from the environment, and 2. privacy. No one I know wears clothes for just those two reasons anymore. True, I know a few people who try, but they're pretty frustrated because it's actually rather impossible.

Consider this: if we once wore wooly mammoth hair to protect

us from the cold winds and to establish a boundary between ourselves and the eyes of our fellow humans, how in the world did we
arrive at:

*Queen
Elizabeth I*

Okay, no one I know wears that either, but I'll return to modern
fashion in a moment. For now, just think about what happened
between the wooly mammoth hair and the crazy queen bling.

Well, what *did* happen?

Fashion happened! The difference between clothing and fashion is that fashion communicates something about the wearer as a
person.[24] My guess is that the moment people realized they had a

....

24 If you want to see a detailed breakdown of the purposes of clothing, check
out *Fashion Design* by Sue Jenkyn Jones (Laurence King, 2005). She elab-
orates on the ideas of "utility, modesty, immodesty, adornment, symbolic
differentiation, social affiliation, psychological self-enhancement, and mod-
ernism." Yes, she's thought very deeply on this matter.

little control over which way a fur hung or what to do with some amazing animal teeth, they reconstituted fit, shape, and accessories according to their personal wishes. This is what I picture:

Caveman: *"Here is your ration of fur until the next hunting season."*

Cave-Mom: *"Thank you, darling. I think I'll create a jaunty hat with this extra bit here."*

Cave-Teen Girl: *"May I have a little tendon and some front teeth to accessorize? Molars are so last year."*

And I also guess that these adaptations happened almost immediately, although I have no scientific data to back me up. Now fast forward a little bit and think of uniforms, religious costumes, or what fashion historians call "ethnic costume."

These kinds of clothes are "fashion" if we define fashion as clothing that communicates something about the personality of the wearer. A uniform denotes a certain job, membership in an organization, or status as a student. Religious garments tell of a faith and can even signal your marital status. Finally, ethnic costume, like a sari or veil, communicates a whole range of messages such as home region, age, marital status, or class.

Of course, when most of us use the word *fashion*, we are referring to the Western notion of *personal* fashion, which began in Europe in the 1200s and spread over time (the notion of personal fashion, not the actual clothes) to just about everywhere around the planet with a few pockets of exceptions.[25] Europe didn't invent the concept of the individual-attempting-control-of-what-she-wore,

....

[25] Intrigued? See Anne Hollender's *Sex and Suits*.

but Western Europe's particular brand of that concept went global after a while, and well, the rest is history.

Ridiculous Fashion

Sometimes we can get caught up with our own times so much we forget that a lot of things are really old problems. For example, what, in heaven's name, inspired Christine de Pizan to say (in 1405), "When a man or a woman sees that someone else is wearing something unusual, then everyone imitates this, just like one sheep follows another . . . in truth, a fool must follow a fool."

Well, ridiculous clothing got her ink to boil. The mob mentality of fashion is as old as time, so it's fun to take a look in history for memorable (to say the least) fashion trends:

Crakow (pointed shoes, or shoes with extended poulaines) were popular in the 1400s and are thought to have originated in Crakow, Poland. They were a little impractical, as the wearer could easily trip and never be able to outrun the enemy on the battlefield. Laws called "sumptuary laws" regulated the length of these shoes so that the nobility's shoes could exceed two feet in length, but peasants' couldn't go beyond six inches. (I can hear the peasants now: "Oh sure that's fine, I don't mind. Besides, you look fab in those, uh, shoes.")

Holy tacos! Don't their necks hurt? Left: Most women of the late eighteenth century (even the most extravagant ones) probably didn't don these babies for anything other than an outrageously special event. But wigs had gotten a little, shall we say, wigged out. Right: This image is entitled "Macaroni" and was a caricature of guys who seriously enjoyed these styles. This is also the age when both men and women were using lead-based powders to give their faces a little poison—I mean, paleness. Men and women also placed fake moles on their faces as well.

Left: "Panniers" of the 1770s. Right: The hoop-skirt of the early 1860s made it difficult for women to go through doorways or not to go up in flames at the fireplace. These examples, like the ones above, show how fashion was used by the upper classes to distinguish themselves from the lower. In other words, it's obviously hard to scrub floors and nurse children while you're buried under hoops of steel.

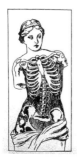
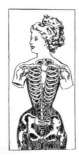

Left: A drawing to caution the ladies about how their organs will be rearranged if they continue to wear the corset. Middle: Two different products for two different kinds of self-mutilation. Right: The lady at last has an S-Shape (and a bad back).

Christine de Pizan lecturing men

Fashion is choice, and behind the word "choice" is the idea that in going for one thing, we didn't go for another. It's a judgment call of sorts and reflects many things about the person making it: sense of self, level of confidence, aspirations, experiences, and especially attitude.

No wonder first impressions are so powerful. We aren't just reading the cover of a book, but also a table of contents and a few choice passages!

Claire McCardell once said *"casual never means careless,"* and it is an appropriate rule of thumb to live by today. It's not surprising that it came from the mid-twentieth-century innovator of American "sportswear," who was nicknamed "Kick" by her three brothers for her ability to stand up to the boys in her life. Claire is considered one of the most influential designers of our American style, and you can detect her ideas in many of the items we wear to today: lightweight skirts, denim, halter necklines, and ballet flats.

HOW TO MAKE A GOOD FIRST IMPRESSION

So, what makes a good first impression? For starters, we never want to look like we've squandered an opportunity to make a smart choice. That wouldn't be, uh, smart. In fact, the choice of what to wear is usually the first choice of the morning and can set the tone of the entire day one way or the other. Then, there's attitude. Showing that we have the appropriate attitude (i.e., we're taking an event seriously, valuing the presence of another person, or respecting a ceremony) is typically easy because each occasion prescribes particular garments. (You don't wear a swimsuit to a job interview unless the job is lifeguarding.) We can also show an appropriate attitude in the way we attend to details such as clean clothes, nails, and hair.

Did I just say, "Showing that we have the appropriate attitude is typically easy because each occasion prescribes particular garments"?

It's not all that easy anymore, is it? Many people have either forgotten the rules for occasion-appropriate dress, or act like they've forgotten them. I've been to a funeral with family members in shorts and flip-flops, and I've seen ripped jeans at a job interview. Then, there's my friend who wears stilettos to picnics. Yes, times have changed, and now people are much more relaxed about rules in general. So, I've taken that into account in writing the list below because standards in fashion should serve people, not the other way around. (Tip: fill in the column entitled "examples from my closet . . .")

WHERE	ATTITUDE	TYPE OF FASHION	EXAMPLES FROM MY CLOSET . . .
At home; at the home of a friend; an overnight stay in a hotel	Relaxed with people you love; kindness to those people through your appearance.	*Personal Casual:* clean and comfortable clothing other than pajamas. (Do not arrive to breakfast in a hotel in your pajamas.)	
In public; running errands to stores, the library, the bank, etc.	Relaxed but focused on purpose; show that you value your time and that you also value the time of the people who assist you.	*Personal Casual:* clean and comfortable clothing other than pajamas or specialized clothing. Bring it up a notch from what you wear at home.	

WHERE	ATTITUDE	TYPE OF FASHION	EXAMPLES FROM MY CLOSET . . .
School (where there is no uniform requirement)	Ready to learn, intelligent, talented, promising, dependable, industrious, adhering to the school dress code.	*School-Appropriate:* skirts, trousers, dress jeans, leggings covered by long tops, and dresses (no short shorts or micro-minis); blouses, shirts, sweaters, and cardigans (no halters, uncovered tanks, or tube tops); flats, boots, tennis shoes, sandals (no flip-flops).	
Work, especially in an office setting or where there is no uniform requirement	Ready to work, intelligent, talented, trustworthy, capable, organized, industrious, adhering to the work dress code.	*Business Casual:* skirts, trousers, dress jeans, and dresses (no shorts); blouses, shirts, sweaters and cardigans (no halters, uncovered tanks, or tube tops); flats, boots, dress sandals (no tennis shoes or flip-flops).	
Work in business or legal environment	Ready to work, intelligent, talented, trustworthy, capable, organized, detail-oriented, industrious, adhering to the work dress code.	*Business:* dress trousers, dress skirts, dresses with jackets or cardigans; blouses, shirts, structured sweaters; suiting; closed-toe pumps, loafers, hosiery; minimal jewelry; covered body art.	

WHERE	ATTITUDE	TYPE OF FASHION	EXAMPLES FROM MY CLOSET
Work in a position of leadership in business environment	Leadership, ready to work, intelligent, talented, trustworthy, capable, organized, detail-oriented, industrious, adhering to the work dress code.	*Corporate or Executive:* Suiting or suit separates; closed-toe pumps, loafers, hosiery; minimal jewelry; covered body art; briefcase.	
Special meals by invitation (restaurant, home, club)	Respect, gratefulness, friendship.	*Celebration Casual:* skirts, trousers, and dresses (no shorts or micro-minis); blouses, shirts, sweaters, and cardigans (no halters, uncovered tanks, or tube tops); flats, loafers, boots, sandals (no flip-flops).	
Ordinary religious observance (Mass, Chapel, Sabbath service)	Respect, reverence.	*Business Casual:* skirts, trousers (check if this is permitted in the venue), and dresses (no shorts or short skirts); cover shoulders with blouses, shirts, sweaters, and cardigans (no halters, uncovered tanks, or tube tops); flats, loafers, boots, sandals with heels (no flip-flops or tennis shoes).	

WHERE	ATTITUDE	TYPE OF FASHION	EXAMPLES FROM MY CLOSET
Extraordinary religious observance or rite of passage (funeral, baptism, naming ceremony, church wedding, bat/bar mitzvah, high holy day)	Respect, reverence, gratitude, joy (baptism, wedding, etc.), or mourning (funeral or memorial service).	*Dressy:* skirts, trousers (check if this is permitted in the venue), and dresses (no shorts or short skirts); cover shoulders with blouses, shirts, sweaters, and cardigans (no halters, uncovered tanks, or tube tops); flats, loafers, boots, sandals with heels (no flip-flops).	
Formal Celebration (evening formal event, wedding reception, retirement dinner)	Respect, gratitude, joy.	*Formal:* long dress (especially for evening formal), ballet flats, dressy sandals or pumps.	
		Semi Formal: dress, skirt and dress blouse, dressy sandals or pumps, heeled boots (in some climates).	
		Cocktail: dress, skirt and dress blouse for early evening to evening hours, dressy sandals or pumps.	

Joe and Rosemary are married! (Thank goodness for my sake.) Grandma is wearing a long, majestic wedding gown which signifies purity (purity of heart, purity of body), solemnity, dignity, grace, and beauty. Even the lilies she carries symbolizes purity and femininity.

So, we can see that conveying an attitude appropriate for the occasion is an essential part of fashion. Yet, there's more to making the right impression, a whole lot more. Can you think? What specifically about your appearance makes a good impression?

The answer goes back to the whole point of connection and communication: *understanding.* So your first impression must help with the person's understanding of you. A good first impression helps the person understand the *best* about you. That seems a tall task for something as flimsy as cloth and peacock feathers, doesn't it? Well, not if you consider *focal point.*

FOCUS ON THIS

and you'll come to understand me

Focal point is the place or area in a field of vision that attracts immediate attention. Think of a beautifully decorated room and consider that in the grand plan, one particular work of art or architectural feature determined the arrangement of furniture, art, plants, and rugs so that it would be highlighted and noticed first. That feature is the room's *focal point.*

What's your focal point at this moment? Think of your outfit and consider where someone's eye goes upon first seeing you. And then, where does it stay?

It could be your feet, true. There are some crazy shoes out there. Or you might have a killer tattoo, which could certainly become a conversation starter. Your breasts? That's a natural focal point for the eyes. Legs? Midriff?

Now consider which part of your physical appearance fosters an understanding of you, the *whole* you. It's your face, especially your eyes.

Your arms, legs, breasts, and earlobes are each wonderfully made and positively beautiful, but they are only parts of you. They don't tell the whole story and your whole story is greater than the sum of your parts.

Therefore, *your face should be the focal point of your fashion.*

Focal point = breast area   *Focal point = hip area*   *Focal point = face!*

If you were to ask someone why she dresses as nicely as she does, she might answer (at least to herself), "so that I look beautiful." What's up with that? What does looking beautiful have to do with focal point?

Think of what beauty is. It's hard to define, isn't it? We can say what we think is beautiful, and even think of beautiful people, but the definition of beauty is hard to put into words. We just seem to know beauty when we see it. When this happens, what we know to be beautiful we also know to be good.[26]

The ancient Greeks spent a lot of time considering the question of what is beautiful. They even came up with a formula called the "Divine Proportion." The gist of it is the notion that a certain arrangement of elements or balance and harmony in an experience is universally attractive to the human person. Obviously, the Greeks could just be speaking for their own kind of thinking, but if you explore widely enough, you'll find that most cultures have some sort of notion that there is beauty in a kind of balance and proportion.

When you remember that we are each attracted to beauty, it's little wonder that we want to be beautiful ourselves. If beauty points to goodness and ultimately to the Truth about our value and purpose, then beauty is indispensable. And, furthermore, the human race couldn't continue without the requisite attraction between the sexes.

So, yes, we want to be beautiful. The well-placed focal point helps the viewer perceive the *whole* beauty of something. Generally,

....

[26] And by "beautiful" I mean authentically "beautiful," not simply glamorous, alluring, or trendy.

if a person perceives your face, he realizes you are a subject, a person with a body and a soul and deserving of the utmost respect. When he perceives your daring cleavage as your obviously chosen focal point, he's thinking about your breasts. It may only last for a few seconds before he makes it to your face, but that's certainly a backwards way to understanding the whole *you*.

Consciously objectifying a person through her shapely legs, full breasts, or stunning hair (or his broad build or winning smile) diminishes the full meaning of beauty. The focus of beauty shifts from the truth about the value of the person to the all-out lie of the body as an object for curiosity, play, or mere admiration.

Turning this idea around, it might be thrilling to know you appear sexy to someone and that's a completely natural desire, but this thrill must transcend an object-oriented understanding of yourself and be placed into the broader context of you as a person with a body and soul, value and purpose. An all-out-sexy look is only good when it's discovered through the meaningful intimacy of sex within marriage.[27] It is not good when the sex that would follow is not in its proper context of a loving marriage.

So, what about a beautiful face? Can't that be used to objectify a person? The answer is yes, as could ankles, hands, or the nape of the neck. You could throw a burka over your body and still be objectified. (Objectification is actually why the burka is there in the first place, but that's another story.)

But your sexual characteristics were also created to be arousing

....

[27] I say "all-out sexy" as in *intentionally head-to-toe sexy*. Often, an innocent, simply feminine characteristic or gesture could be found to be "sexy." In modern English, that's not as loaded a word as it used to be.

to a man. Remember, a guy is also a human person with a Dignity, distinction, and freedom, just like you. You both have the responsibility to connect, communicate, and understand within the context of a mutually respectful relationship. He has the freedom to look away from your breasts to your face (and therefore everything else about you) and acknowledge your full value, and he can do this with an appreciation for your breasts and hips and legs because those curves speak about love and life. He can do this, but you should not communicate to him that you want his attention to remain only on your breasts.

It might seem unfair and a bit baffling that it is your responsibility to help redirect his attention to the whole you, but his brain pathways are wired differently than yours are. His visual sensors are very sensitive. (This is how males get addicted to porn more easily than females.) True, if we women had to conceal every possibly arousing or exciting feature of our bodies, then we could never interact with men at all! So, rather than taking a defensive, damage-control approach in the pursuit of preventing inappropriate glances, we should work from the positive understanding that a guy needs to see your whole person through his focus on your face, especially your eyes. Through your person-oriented connection and subsequent understanding, he can come to respect your value and purpose (and motivations, aspirations, talents, opinions, and intelligence).

Keep the focal point on your face:

1. Stand up straight and hold your head high. Look your listener in the eyes.

2. Accent your eyes with a little eye makeup, especially mascara.

3. Use makeup with the strategy of placing the focal point on the eyes. Blush isn't about red cheeks; it's about lifting the cheekbone and directing attention to the eyes. Foundation evens out skin tone to offset the eyes. Lipstick, if applied not to compete with the eyes, can provide a nice counterweight to them.

4. Wear a hairstyle that frames your face and keeps your hair out of your eyes.

5. Choose accessories that frame the face. Earrings do this instantly. A necklace, a string of necklaces, or a scarf are also nice touches. Also, take special care in choosing a pair of eyeglasses, as these should allow people to see your eyes without hindrance.

6. Choose a neckline that complements your face shape. Collars are universally flattering. Scoop-necks help to soften hard jaw lines, and v-necks help to elongate shorter necks.

7. Avoid showing the skin around and between your breasts.

8. Wear a bra that gives support and nipple coverage. Keep straps hidden.

9. Consider your entire look in front of a full-length mirror. Where does the eye land along your image? Flashes of skin or tightness of fabric work like competing focal points for your face. Avoid baring the midriff or sporting super-short skirts or shorts.

10. Minimize piercing around the face and generally avoid tattoos.

I always think that the best way to dress is when the person notices you first and the dress after.

— OSCAR DE LA RENTA —

designer known for extraordinary fashion

VAIN ATTEMPTS

"TWO chapters on dressing well?" you may ask, "Isn't all this attention to appearances a kind of vanity?"

Brava, dear reader! You've been reading this book closely. (Maybe you've peeked at that long chart in Chapter 6!) But the answer is *not unless you allow it.*

Vanity is a vice that is defined as an excessive pride in one's appearance. The word "excessive" implies that there can indeed be at least a little pride (i.e., self-respect). If you read a dictionary entry for the word all the way to the end, you'll also see that vanity implies a "uselessness" or "worthlessness" because the pride is only about show and façade. So, if I'm excessively concerned about my appearance, I can appear to be mostly show with little substance. (Talk about *not* keeping my true value and purpose right in front and center!)

How do you know when you are vain about your fashion? If you find yourself always thinking about it, constantly checking yourself in the mirror, comparing yourself to others, or spending way too much time and money on looking better, you are behaving in a *vain* way. My advice: get your mind off this kind of thinking and consider how you can do something for someone else (an unexpected favor, a gift, or a kindness). Selfless actions are a sure-fire cure for any anxiety about how you look.

The five-minute makeup miracle
and it looks like you're not wearing any makeup at all!

It's a rite of passage (and kind of a human right, really) to know how to put on makeup properly.

Do these steps in natural light with a mirror that reflects your entire face.

On a clean and moisturized face, dab concealer onto blemishes and any other marks that can be concealed. Blend lightly. Dab foundation on each cheek, on the tip of the nose, and on the forehead. Then, in a circular motion with your index and middle finger (or foundation brush or sponge), blend completely. (This will also blend in the concealer.) Check that the color blends into the neck. Blend from the upper lip into the nostril so that skin tone in that area is even.

Add blush with a blush brush from directly under the eye upward to the temple. Ensure that the blush doesn't look like stripes. Next, if you like, add a light powder over the entire face. This should be applied with a bronzer brush.

Turn to your eyes. Using a light pink, vanilla, or "nude" powder, fill in the entire lid up to the brow bone. Next, add a

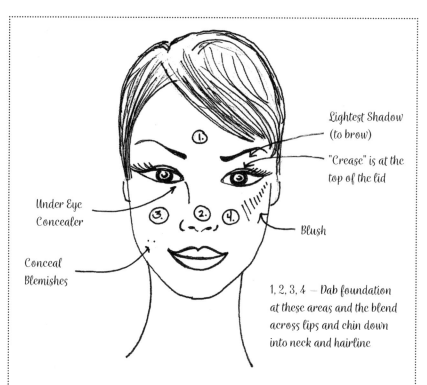

Lightest Shadow
(to brow)

"Crease" is at the
top of the lid

Under Eye
Concealer

Blush

Conceal
Blemishes

1, 2, 3, 4 — Dab foundation
at these areas and the blend
across lips and chin down
into neck and hairline

mid-tone color like a mauve or a light gray to the lid from the lash line to the crease. Finally, add a darker color such as a taupe or brown into the crease. Line the lashline with eyeliner pencil on the top lid from a quarter of the way out from the nose to the outer eye. Do the same to the bottom lash line. Fill in brows if necessary. Add mascara in such a way that the wand goes in slow motion, "grabbing" the lashes, holding them outward and upward for two seconds. Do this twice.

Add a light color to lips with either a lipstick or a gloss. For a special occasion, and to enlarge the lips, use liner on the outside line of the lips, fill in, and add lipstick on top.

SENSE AND SENSIBILITY

and how to shop well

A lot of clothing on the fashion market does not always meet everyone's ideal of beauty. Obviously, clothing manufacturers know that women buy clothing for other reasons besides beauty enhancement. There's novelty, shock-value, artistry, and others too numerous to mention. This isn't anything new; just look at the fashion history described earlier in the chapter.

I said earlier that you know beauty when you see it, but in that shopping moment, "fitting in," or getting a look we think is trendy and cool, we sometimes ignore all sense of Divine Proportion, or any other kind of sense.

Don't you sometimes look into your closet and wonder, *"What was I thinking?"*

Don't feel too badly; fashion marketers spend billions of dollars attempting to convince you that you must buy their goods. How do they do this?

Let's consider this scenario:

It's Saturday afternoon and Marianne is thrilled to have just found a wonderful present for her sister, Elinor. Elinor's birthday party is in just a few hours, so Marianne is in a good mood; she's thinking about her sister's surprise at the gift, looking forward to seeing a particular guy, and excited to sport the outfit she bought recently online. Her car is just outside of Snooties Department Store, so she heads into the store through its fancy mall entrance, thinking she is finished with all her shopping.

But within seconds she smells a perfume that reminds her of a beautiful person she knows. Then, there's an enlarged (and airbrushed and edited) photo of an unbelievably gorgeous model. There's another one, and another. "Whoa!" *Marianne thinks,* "Check out that gorgeous skin. Is my skin anything like that? Are my eyes at all like those? I bet she has no problem at parties . . . or anywhere else for that matter. Do I even look a little bit like her?"

And then the very beautiful Marianne passes a mirror. "No," *she answers,* "Sadly, I do not look anything like her."

And her prior happiness reconstitutes itself into a plan for an extreme makeover: "First, a visit to the makeup counter, then shoes, and possibly a skirt or two."

OH MARIANNE!

Don't you have any sense?

Maybe for you (or Marianne's sensible sister Elinor), your thought process in a store isn't as transparent as what I just related. However, these thoughts happen to most people on at least a subconscious level. Fashion marketing tells a story—a myth, really—and invites you to be a part of it. Let's break it down: **the "Story,"** the **myth** that **Marianne** believes, and the sensible **response** that **Elinor** (or maybe you or I) might have when we are thinking clearly.

The Story: These women in these t-shirts are gorgeous; they're smiling and having fun at a coffee shop in some sophisticated city like New York or Paris.

Marianne: Maybe I too could be gorgeous and smiling and having fun if I buy a t-shirt with that very same logo on it.

Elinor: It's only a t-shirt. It's not worth $29.99. Why give this company free advertising by wearing its logo? They should pay me to do something like that.

The Story: These women in these bikinis are beautiful and smiling at the volleyball net while the gorgeous, smiling guys are hovering over them.

Marianne: The guys might hover over me if I get waxed, hit the tanning salon, and get that hot pink string bikini.

Elinor: Three triangles of cloth might get the guys to hover, but not in a way that appreciates me as me.

The Story: Angelina Fox, the star of "Lifestyles of the Desperate," knows everything about fashion, including how to choose a great pair of sunglasses.

Marianne: People will think that I know everything about fashion if I wear the same sunglasses she does.

Elinor: No pair of non-prescription sunglasses is worth $169.99.

The Story: This store, with the loud club music, the dim lighting, and the photos of unbelievably gorgeous guys is THE place to see and be seen.

Marianne: Buying even a pair of socks from this place will make me sexy, solve my problems, and get me friends.

Elinor: Socks might keep my feet warm. Um, that's all.

IT'S ONLY A T-SHIRT

If I entitled this paragraph with the word "business," you'd probably prepare yourself for an important message. You'd think about money, important people who make decisions about money, and more money. You'd also think about opportunity and the stress that comes with your not wanting to miss out on anything.

But I chose the title "It's only a t-shirt" because after all, the hype advertising builds up around one product is dissolved by the next big thing (perhaps another t-shirt), and then you're left with just a t-shirt!

Fashion *is* business—big business. Fashion knows it is business and it knows its business. Do we take ourselves at least as seriously as the brand takes itself? Often not, as we sometimes buy our clothing with a little more admiration for the brand name than for ourselves as persons, and we place more trust in the aesthetic judgement of the designers than what they may deserve from us.

Part of the reason that we are taken in by advertising is because we are lulled into the illusion that there's never much money involved. It's only a twenty-five-dollar blouse here or a forty-dollar pair of shoes there. The problem is that this money all adds up over time, so that we end up with a closetful of items that aren't fit for our mission of personal communication (i.e., fashion).

A client of mine had this habit of buying things and then changing her mind about them once they hit the closet. She just couldn't bring herself to return anything, even after she decided not to wear it. Once she hired me for help, we totaled a whopping $1,240 worth of unreturned merchandise. Think of all the things she could have done with that money.

On the other hand, fashion is about art and self-expression, and it's a tool for communication. It is perfectly appropriate to spend *some* money on clothing. (And I've had plenty of clients who had serious anxiety about doing that too.) Here's how to spend money on clothes in a way that can eliminate any guilt:

1. Establish a reasonable budget for your clothing. Write down an amount that you think might work (considering your lifestyle, your allowance or pay, and where you shop), and try sticking to the budget.

2. Read the next chapter thoroughly and come up with a shopping plan.

3. Do not use shopping as entertainment. Meet friends at places other than a mall or a shopping venue if the sight of merchandise is just too much of a temptation.

4. Use only cash for shopping, even planned shopping. Use credit only if you've proven to yourself that you can stick to your budget.

5. In a "marketing moment" (you see a bus with a cool ad, you're passing the makeup counter of *Snooties*, you're scrolling through *Amazon*, you see an episode of "Lifestyles of the Desperate," or you're reading the latest post of *In Step* Magazine), reduce the message to its core: *it's just a white t-shirt; it's only a dress; the handbag in question is cute but will break in one season.*

6. Don't pull tags off garments until you put them on for the day. If you decide not to keep something, return it immediately.

7. Keep a file of receipts. I keep mine in my purse and then transfer them to an envelope at the end of the month.

8. Write experience notes for shopping. Note which venues (online and offline) work and which don't. Keep track of the best websites and understand their return policies and shipping costs.

CHAPTER 4

Look at Me!

Personal Fashion Choices

Anne Elliot spent her high school years following a strict dress code that often rankled her sense of freedom. In college she got sloppy for class but enjoyed wearing colorful scarves, dressing up on weekends, and occasionally finding cute shoes to wear for her part-time job. Now, she's landed her first full-time job in advertising and she's surrounded by coworkers who seem to be enamored with an eclectic mix of high fashion, motorcycle gangs, and 80s rockers. Anne's been subtly persuaded to change her style, and has ditched her pencil skirts for pleather leggings, her ballet flats for high-heeled platform booties, and her sweaters for statement t-shirts and cheap fast-fashion bling.

It's now Monday morning and Anne is looking in her closet. It's dawned on her that she's spent more time thinking about her work clothing than her actual work, and is suddenly uninspired by what's hanging before her. She's asking herself, "Is any of this really me?"

IT'S NOT SO ME AFTER ALL

Poor Anne is not alone in her fashion dilemma. Don't most of us stray away from our instincts in a sudden fit of admiration for another woman's style?

Yes, most of us do at some point. We copy the fashions of others because we want to fit in or make a statement, or because we find something flattering, or for all of these reasons because fashion is what we use to connect, communicate, and be understood.

Picture your closet as it stands right now. Go ahead, close your eyes and imagine it. Now imagine yourself reaching in and pulling out something that you just never seem to be in the mood to wear. (There are a few of those things, aren't there?)

Take a good look at this item. It might be flattering, kind of pretty, and maybe even an awesome color, but you just never go for it. You're never "in the mood" for it. It hangs there as a reminder that you really "have nothing to wear."

It's all a case of mistaken fashion identity. You thought it would work when you decided to keep it, but your gut instinct prevents you from ever wearing it. There are probably several other things in your closet just like this piece. Not understanding your fashion personality can become expensive, if you keep buying clothes that you'll never use.

Caroline Herrera is a woman who seemed to know her fashion personality from a very young age. Born in Caracas, Venezuela but working from New York, she is now a retired fashion designer who became famous for elegance and tasteful creativity over her thirty-seven years of prolific fashion merchandising. She's dressed Jackie Kennedy Onassis, Laura Bush, Michelle Obama, and Melania Trump,  and many celebrities in Hollywood without losing any of her original warmth and freshness. She's an example of a fashion influence who helps others find their own fashion personalities.

Carolina Herrera is one of several fashion influences I've come to admire over the years. I get the feeling that she really enjoys being a woman.

How do you find *your* fashion personality? Most people figure it out by studying what works for them and what doesn't. A nice shortcut is the two-part test below. Try answering each question with your gut reaction.

FASHION PERSONALITY PART 1:

the inspiration

Answer each question concerning what you admire and enjoy about fashion. This section involves your ideal style, not necessarily what you currently own right now.

1. My dream wardrobe would be:

a. *comfortable and easy to maintain, despite how hard I can be on my clothing.*

b. *sweet and down to earth (like me at my best). It wouldn't involve too much effort.*

c. *an inspired result of an artistic and responsible use of materials. It would be lovely.*

d. *elegant and feminine. It would be filled with high-quality pieces and accessories.*

e. *absolutely fashion-forward and flattering for me.*

f. *head-turning and memorable.*

2. Qualities I need in my clothing:

a. *ease of movement, unstructured styles, and lean lines that flatter my shape.*

b. *versatility, attractiveness, and the freedom to feel completely at ease.*

c. *uniqueness, creativity, a touch of romance.*

d. *tastefulness, lines that flatter my shape, attention to details, and high quality.*

e. *inspiration and trendiness.*

f. *glamour.*

3. I might think of the following when considering my favorite styles:

a. *dancers, athletes.*

b. *the countryside, outdoor enthusiasts.*

c. *bohemians, artists, poets.*

d. *royalty, icons of fashion, first ladies, diplomats.*

e. *fashion professionals, visual artists, celebrities.*

f. *singers, stage performers, iconic celebrities.*

4. I'd most likely be inspired by:

a. *sports photography, Olympic champions, the ballet, modern dance.*

b. *folk or country musicians, "real" fashion around me, maybe some vintage fashion.*

c. *images from history, images from other cultures, folk art.*

d. *images of famous "ladies," vintage photos, some haute couture.*

e. *fashion magazines, "street fashion" features, runway fashion, travel.*

f. *fashion magazines, images of entertainers, glamorous vintage photos.*

5. An "inspiration board" for my general tastes would include:

a. the human form, movement, photos of nature (especially with water).

b. landscapes (both soft and rugged), flowers, animals, quaint homes, nostalgic sites.

c. difficult to find destinations, things that grow, folk art.

d. photographs of elegant people, art, architecture, décor, precious stones, high-class destinations.

e. current style icons, art (the mainstream and the obscure), popular music, décor, graphic arts.

f. show business, favorite music and musicians, current style icons, photographs of grand places, exotic destinations.

6. An "inspiration board" for clothing for me would include:

a. performance wear, athleisure, comfortable footwear, body-conforming handbags or backpacks.

b. denim, sweaters, t-shirts, maybe cowboy boots.

c. skirts, dresses, charming accessories, exotic add-ons.

d. something cashmere, pencil skirts, iconic dresses, great shoes and handbags.

e. anything and everything and it would need to be updated constantly.

f. high-heeled shoes, some dresses, shiny stuff, and I'd squeeze in a section for makeup.

7. *The best compliment for my style would be:*

a. "Her style is low key but graceful."

b. "Her style is genuine and pretty."

c. "Her style is unique and creative."

d. "Her style is elegant and polished."

e. "Her style is innovative and exciting."

f. "Her style is glamorous and sophisticated."

YOUR INSPIRATION

is seen in your muse.

I'm sure you've heard of the muses from Greek mythology. Now, imagine how the muse, this mythical woman who inspires artists, writers, and musicians, might inspire a fashion designer or stylist. Hubert de Givenchy had Audrey Hepburn, Oleg Cassini had Jackie Kennedy, and these days you see the likes of Victoria Beckham designing specifically for an actress like Gwyneth Paltrow. Maybe you know someone who watches the magazines for a current fashion icon, or you've heard that your great-aunt Alice was inspired by Grace Kelly or Lucille Ball.

But a muse doesn't have to be an heiress or a celebrity. Unlike the down-in-the-trenches fashion designer who needs the patronage (and extra attention), you can choose a muse who is a *compilation* of your favorite things in life. This muse reflects how you desire to use fashion as a tool for communicating your tastes, your talents, and your aspirations.

So, if you answered mostly "a", your muse might be the ATHLETE or DANCER. You are inspired by movement in athletics and dance. You look for graceful lines, breathable fabrics, and simple combinations. You dislike any fuss or over-embellishment, and enjoy having a single outfit work for the entire day.

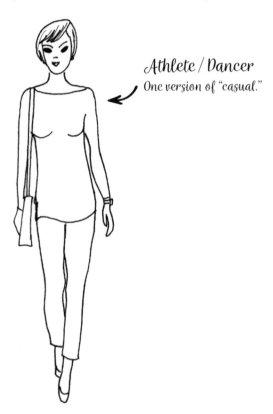

Athlete / Dancer
One version of "casual."

Your Strength: You keep things simple.

Your Pitfall: You might get sloppy.

If you answered mostly "b", your muse might be the GIRL NEXT DOOR. You are inspired by the beauty of the country, hard work, and interesting old-fashioned objects. You like to look fresh, comfortable, and approachable. You'd rather not have the all the attention drawn to you, and you dislike pretension and show.

Girl Next-Door
One version of "casual."

Your Strength: You know how to coordinate.

Your Pitfall: You might get bored with your clothing. *One version of "casual."*

If you answered mostly "c", your muse might be the DREAMER.
You are inspired by all things beautiful, both the ephemeral (like
a blooming flower, an inspirational piece of music, or the feel of a
texture) and the long-lasting (like the landscape or a work of art).
You enjoy softer lines, exotic details, and "beautiful" colors.

Dreamer
One version of "casual."

Your Strength: You are creative and at your best you are inspiring
to others.

Your Pitfall: You may have difficulty translating your inspiration
for professional settings.

If you answered mostly "d", your muse might be the LADY. You are inspired by strong classic designs in art, architecture, and fashion. You might appreciate the off-beat, but you tend to return to the mainstream things you know and love. You enjoy high-quality items, maintaining decorum, and living the social graces. You wouldn't like to be called *pretentious*, but you'd get over it because you'd know that being a lady isn't about pretension or show.

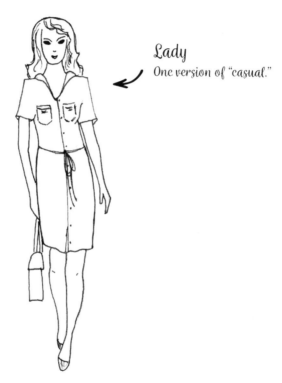

Lady
One version of "casual."

Your Strength: You pay attention to details and often get it "right."

Your Pitfall: You often resist change and updates.

If you answered mostly "e", your muse might be the FASHION PLATE. You are the artist and fashion is your art form. You enjoy the act of creation and you're always looking for the next big thing in fashion and style. You can find inspiration almost anywhere, which is why you're such a trendsetter.

Fashion Plate
One version of "casual."

Your Strength: You have confidence in your fashion.

Your Pitfall: You can over-do it sometimes.

If you answered mostly "f", your muse might be the DIVA. You like being the center of attention (but you're working on your humility) and you can turn almost any occasion into a reason for dressing your best. You are inspired by entertainment (Vaudeville, Broadway, Hollywood), music, city life, and beautiful people.

Diva
One version of "casual."

Your Strength: You enjoy the "tools" of fashion and being a woman.

Your Pitfall: You may sometimes choose inappropriate fashions.

WHERE IS MY MUSE ON A MONDAY MORNING?

Inspiration is one thing, shopping is another. Then, there's the whole issue of *lifestyle*. For example, your muse might be the **Lady**, but your long walk across the campus does away with your idea of cute shoes for at least five days of the week. Your mom might have been the **Dreamer** in her day, but as with many mothers, has moved on to live out other dreams.

That's okay. And it's why there is a second part to our fashion personality test.

FASHION PERSONALITY PART 2:

Approach to Fashion

Now that you know what inspires you, it's time to reflect on how you actually live out your sense of fashion.

1. My approach to color is:

a. *I've never had an approach. I guess I choose what's on sale at my usual places or what I think might hide stains.*

b. *I'm limited to what's available in my usual stores. I try to choose flattering colors, but sometimes I don't because the items with unflattering colors happen to be the less expensive choices, or I just don't have time to keep looking and so I give up.*

c. *I find out what looks best on me and try to plan a wardrobe around those colors. I don't buy something unless I really like it.*

d. *I just buy the colors I'm inspired to buy. No looking back.*

2. *I consider accessories to be:*

a. *Anything other than a top or a bottom and I barely think about those.*

b. *Critical. My shoes and my bag must work hard for me and I'm willing to give up style so that I'm at my most efficient.*

c. *An integral part of a wardrobe and a great way to express myself. I choose the accessories that are both functional and stylish most of the time.*

d. *Icing on the cake! I love to go for all the things I absolutely love no matter the cost.*

3. *When a new fashion season approaches, I plan for it by:*

a. *Huh? Plan?*

b. *Well, if I happen to have time, I'll look around, but ultimately, I'm not going out of my way to do anything. I'll probably buy things on sale.*

c. *I preview the season a little bit. I come up with a list based upon my needs (even if it's only in my head) and I make shopping a priority.*

d. *Not only do I preview the season, write a list, and make shopping a priority, but I can't be bothered with anything else while I'm on it! Often, I'll throw away the list and just go for something I absolutely must have.*

4. My fashion budget is:

a. What? Budget?

b. Whatever is left over after rent, groceries, and school stuff. If there's no money left over, then I'll figure out how to make the clothes I have work for me. Hopefully. When I get around to it.

c. I have an actual line in my budget for fashion purchases (at least in my head). In financially tight seasons, I look for alternative venues like discount, off-pricers, or secondhand.

d. A budget only stifles true inspiration.

5. At this point in time, my feeling toward my wardrobe is:

a. Apathy. Lukewarm vibes on a good day.

b. That it's been one big compromise. I have to settle for things that aren't really me.

c. It's so me! I take pleasure and pride in my wardrobe.

d. It changes constantly. Sometimes I'm thrilled and at other times, I can visualize something even better.

If you answered mostly "a", you have a RELUCTANT approach to your fashion. Take the word *reluctant* and place it before your muse: ***the reluctant* _____** (*Athlete, Girl Next Door, Dreamer, Lady, Fashion Plate, Diva*) *is my fashion personality.*

This means that fashion is not a high priority for you. You may want it to be (or not), or maybe it once was, but right now you are bit passive and unresponsive to your muse.

Tips: Put aside time for your clothing choices. Reflect on what inspires you (maybe this test helped you) and keep a record of the things you do find kind of attractive.

If you answered mostly "b", you take a PRACTICAL approach to your fashion. Take the word *practical* and place it before your muse: ***the practical*** _____ (*Athlete, Girl Next Door, Dreamer, Lady, Fashion Plate, Diva*) ***is my fashion personality.***

You value looking your best, but you have so many other priorities right now that fashion often takes you by surprise. You may not be passive, but you are trying your best under the circumstances.

Tips: If you made time to read this book, you've taken a step in the right direction.

If you answered mostly "c", you have a THOUGHTFUL approach to your fashion. Take the word *thoughtful* and place it before your muse: ***the thoughtful*** _____ (*Athlete, Girl Next Door, Dreamer, Lady, Fashion Plate, Diva*) ***is my fashion personality.***

You are very self-aware and enjoy your fashion. You don't blindly run into the store, choosing whatever happens to be the latest fashion, but consider your own needs first.

Tips: You've got it girl!

If you answered mostly "d", you have a GUNG-HO approach to your fashion. Take the word *gung-ho* and place it before your muse: ***the gung-ho*** _____ (*Athlete, Girl Next Door, Dreamer, Lady, Fashion Plate, Diva*) ***is my fashion personality.***

You are a truly inspired person. However, you may get so absorbed in your clothing choices that you may not be getting to the more important things in life.

Tips: Become more reflective and methodical in your fashion decisions, and think about your real needs before you consider the "must-haves."

A *Gung-ho Diva, Thoughtful Lady,* or *Practical Dreamer?*[28]

Don't see it as a label—see it as a challenge! I certainly don't mean to categorize you, but the nice thing about choosing a muse is that you can change it over time. You may decide that you like something completely different from what you've found here.

What if I picked every kind of muse? That could mean that you are open-minded and you just like everything. Consider what you like best of all. Or, it could be that you are indeed a *fashion plate* and like to reinvent looks according to your moods.

What if I tied for two or even three muses? Review your answers and narrow them down to two. You can consider your muse a combination of the ones listed here. (There is no right or wrong answer with this, so for example, one could be a "practical athlete–fashion plate" or a "thoughtful dreamer–lady" or "lady–dreamer.")[29]

What if I don't like any of these muses? Then come up with your own muse. It could be a lot of fun and that's the point!

What about Anne at the office? At her new job, she's behaving like the *Gung-Ho Fashion Plate* while in the past, she'd been a *Reluctant Lady*. If she's taken the test above, she may find that she can become the *Thoughtful Lady* and update her pieces so she feels current and creative. It is most likely her "office culture" of creativity and statement-making that inspired her to change into something she didn't want to be.

---

[28] You may have noticed that some descriptors don't really go along with some types of inspiration. For example, there are probably very few "reluctant fashion plates" because being a fashion plate requires a bit of enthusiasm.

[29] I'm a "Thoughtful Lady–Fashion Plate." Can't you tell?

Who is my real-life muse?

As you can imagine, I get asked this a lot!

As is the case for most people, several individuals inspire me. Most of them are women I know very well, and, in fact, one of them is a client of mine. She's so creatively elegant that I wonder why she's not *my* stylist! If pressed to name someone famous, I could mention Audrey Hepburn, Kate Middleton, or Livia Firth, but the one person whose style captures my imagination has been gone from this world for over thirty years, the actress Ingrid Bergman.

I'm savvy enough to know that I should never copy her exactly, but I do enjoy seeing old photos of her.

THREE ELEMENTS OF STYLE

Congratulations! You just completed a process that I facilitate with each client in my fashion-consulting business. Fashion personality is one of three things that I call the "Elements of Style."

To get the most out of this chapter and to make real changes in your wardrobe, continue to take notes below, roll up your sleeves, and get into that closet of yours!

GO FIGURE!

you've got one and it's beautiful.

Let's continue with the next Element of Style: **proportion in your silhouette.**

The dress must follow the body of a woman, not the body following the shape of the dress."

— HUBERT DE GIVENCHY —
a classy fashion designer from the 1950s

Remember the discussion on balance and proportion? Well, these elements take a very real form in something called your *silhouette*. Your silhouette is the outline or shape of your entire appearance from a frontal view, and most often refers to the ensemble (outfit) itself.

So, through the twentieth century, we've had several dominant silhouettes:

| 1910s | 1920s | 1940s | 1950s | 1960's |

(Women of these eras didn't have bodies shaped any differently from ours; these silhouettes are aesthetics that inspired women to create the optical illusion of these shapes.)

Each look above worked in its time because of context and expectation. These days, no one part of the body is emphasized, so one's top and bottom appear about the same size (balanced) even though the majority of women aren't. (The majority of women have naturally larger bottom halves.)

If you are old enough to read this book (and if you aren't a guy), you have curves. You are supposed to have curves. Curves are beautiful. Curves signify life, and life is good.

Your curves could be around your bottom half, where most women have them. Or your curves are at your shoulders and breasts. Or your top and bottom are about the same size and you might have a bit of curviness in your tummy. Or you're waiting for your curves to happen.

Let's locate your natural volume:

If you wear a larger size on the bottom than you do on the top, your natural volume is in your hip area. Your buttocks and your upper thighs are where your curves are.

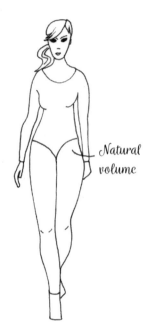

Natural volume

Natural volume

If you wear a larger size on top than you do on the bottom, your natural volume is in your breast/rib cage area. You might also have broad shoulders.

If you wear the same size on top as you do on the bottom (e.g., a size eight for shirts and a size eight for pants) you have top-bottom balance. Your natural volume may be mostly in your waist or tummy. Or, maybe you don't have much natural volume.

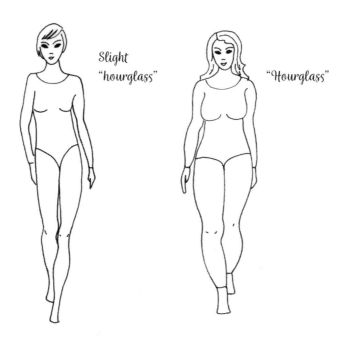

Slight "hourglass"

"Hourglass"

CREATING THE OPTICAL ILLUSION OF PROPORTION

So, what do we mean by *proportion*? Currently, despite the tubular shape of high-fashion models or the bustiness of lingerie models, the aesthetic is for a woman's top and bottom to be about the same size, with an indentation at the waist. (The top-bottom balance silhouette is the guiding shape the garment industry uses for design.) So, if the bust, the bottom, or the tummy appears to be disproportionately larger than the rest of the body, that part may serve as a competing focal point to the face. If you doubt that, think of the last time you saw someone's buttocks squeezed into a too-tight pair of leggings. Now try to remember her face. See what I mean?

You could say that the inspirational shape for fashion design is an hourglass:

Most women don't mirror this hourglass shape standing unaided in their birthday suit. (Remember, no matter what the guiding aesthetic, lots of people won't naturally have that silhouette.) They can do a few little tricks with their wardrobe to get that balance and proportion. The following are some timeless tips I give to my clients:

1. ***A particular style creates a particular silhouette.*** Choose the garment according to where you want to add a little artificial volume and help streamline where you already have natural volume.

Balance:
a dress that adds artificial volume to the bottom, opposite her natural volume on top

Balance:
a dress that adds artificial volume to the top, opposite her natural volume on the bottom

2. *Coordinate color to give the illusion of proportion:* Light colors add artificial volume. Darker colors streamline. So, a white shirt over a black pair of pants, or a powder-pink sweater over a pair of dark blue jeans would give balance to someone whose curviness is in the hips.

Likewise, a black or navy top over a light-colored or white bottom would give balance to someone whose curviness is in the bust.

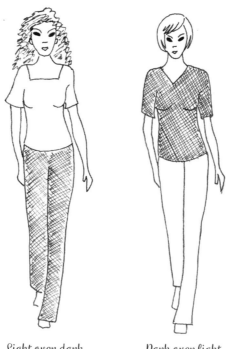

Light over dark   Dark over light

3. *Use line to give the illusion of proportion:* Horizontal lines add
   the look of greater volume. Vertical lines create a streamlined
   look. So, a rugby shirt will add artificial volume to your top
   while streamlining the appearance of your hips.

Diagonal lines that are more horizontal add volume. Diagonal
lines that are more vertical streamline.

That means that **monochromatic looks**
create a vertical line, elongating the entire
look.

*Monochromatic makes
a strong vertical line*

4. ***Play print/pattern off solids to create the illusion of proportion.*** Prints and patterns add volume, especially when placed
opposite of solids.

Exception: the swimsuit. When fabric like spandex form-fits the
body, print aids the eyes by "skimming over" any bit of volume
underneath.

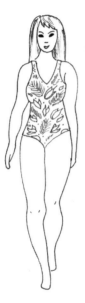

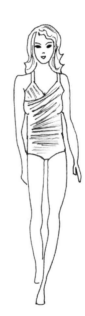

| Print works with natural curves | Ruffle adds artificial volume to top | Diagonal lines minimize top | High neckline and horizontal lines add artificial volume to top, adding balance |

5. ***Play thicker or shiny fabrics off thinner or matte ones to create the illusion of proportion.*** Fabrics with a thicker nap (boucle, velvet, fleece, etc.) add volume. Fabrics with any kind of sheen or an embellishment will also add volume.

6. ***Simple, clean areas will streamline.*** Detailed or "cluttered" areas add volume. So, strategically place pockets, pleats, zippers, folds, ruching, ruffles, lace, buttons, or embroidery.

Clean and lean line

Details add artificial volume to top

7. ***Have a working relationship with your undergarments.*** A bra should support your breasts and shouldn't be noticeably tight- or loose-fitting. Padding in a bra adds volume where you may need it to help a structured top fit better.

   And, although it might seem like ancient history, there is this great invention called *panty hose.* This fabulous tool gives a smooth look, keeps legs warm in the winter, and helps your garments keep a clean line throughout.

8. ***Finally, rely on your favorite accessories to add fun to your wardrobe.*** A well-placed scarf or exactly the right size handbag can help create the optical illusion of proportion at least as much as a well-chosen silhouette or patterned blouse. And anyway, accessories are mostly about personality and meant to be enjoyed!

FUN WITH COLOR

free and curiously satisfying

The third Element of Style is **color palette**. A color palette is the group or family of colors that looks best on you because they make your skin glow, your lips pinker, and your eyes twinkle. The right color palette achieves the same goal that great makeup does.

There are four color palettes: *Cool, Light Cool, Warm, Light Warm.*

Cool	Warm
Blue-toned, bright, intense, "gem tones," primary colors, black, and white	*Golden-toned, muted, "autumn" colors, warm browns and yellow creams*
Light Cool	**Light Warm**
All cool colors lightened with white, "chalky" white, grays	*All warm colors lightened with white, some bright, some soft*

So, color from the **cool** palette is any color with a bit of blue in it, like that "deep brick" red that gets close to the color of wine. A red that looks more like the color of a tomato is a **warm** red. It has a hint of yellow in it.

A **light-cool** color is just a cool color that has white added (a tint). So, mauve and pink are light-cool versions of red. A **light-warm** color is a warm color that's lighter. So, salmon would be a light-warm version of red. (Okay, maybe a distant cousin of red.) One of these colors is the BEST color for you. That best color is part of a whole *palette of colors.*

You find your best color palette by testing colors against your face. Here's how:

1. Gather together (from your closet—and your dad's, mom's, sisters', and brothers' closets) the following colors and group them into these categories:[30]

COOL COLORS	LIGHT COOL COLORS	WARM COLORS	LIGHT WARM COLORS
White	***	Cream	***
Black	Gray like the sky before rain	***	***
***	***	Brown like "stained oak" furniture	Khaki or beige
Bright red like the red of the flag	Medium pink like rose	Orange like a pumpkin	Light orange like salmon
Deep blue like cobalt	Sky blue	***	***
***	***	Olive green	Celery green
Purple like a grape or *Barney the Dinosaur*	Violet	***	***
***	***	Yellow like French mustard	Yellow like a banana peel

....

[30] The three asterisks (***) on this chart do not indicate that such a category ("warm blue" or "light warm blue") does not exist, it merely indicates that it might be difficult to actually find that color in your home. I didn't want to discourage you by telling you to search for it.

2. ***Next, grab a large mirror and take it outside or into a well-lighted room.*** You might want to also grab an honest friend while you're at it. (This process is even more fun with friends.)

3. ***Hold up just two types of colors below your face: Cool vs. Warm.*** First, hold up the cool color. Then hold up the warm color. Compare how they look. Which one is better? If you can't tell, give your eyes a quick break by placing a color on your shoulders, looking away (and switching the colors while your eyes are away from mirror) then looking back at the second color. (You'll see that one is at least slightly better than the other.)

Circle each one that looks better on the chart below. This determines your need for either Cool or Warm colors.

COOL COLORS	WARM COLORS
White	Cream
Black	Brown like "stained oak"
Bright red like the one in the flag	Orange like a pumpkin
Deep blue	Olive green
Purple like a grape or *Barney the Dinosaur*	Yellow like French mustard

4. *Make a decision. If the cool colors look better*, then you require a cool palette. It may be, however, that you need these cool colors a bit lighter. *This time, compare each cool color to each light cool color.* Whichever looks better is your color palette.

COOL COLORS	LIGHT COOL COLORS
White	*(There's really no such thing as a "lighter" white. A chalky, off-white would be a good tester opposite white.)*
Black	Gray
Bright red like the one in the flag	Medium pink like a rose
Deep blue	Sky blue
Purple like a grape or Barney	Violet

The Color Palette that's most flattering for me is

....

5. **ON THE OTHER HAND**, if the warm colors look better, you require a warm palette. It may be, however, that you need these warm colors a bit lighter. *This time, compare each warm color to each light warm color.* Whichever looks better is your color palette.

WARM COLORS	LIGHT WARM COLORS
Cream	*(A light cream or "ivory" would be a good tester opposite cream.)*
Brown like "stained oak"	Khaki or beige
Orange like a pumpkin	Light orange like the flesh of a peach
Olive green	Celery green
Yellow like mustard	Yellow like a banana

The Color Palette that's most flattering for me is

....

So, you've got a closet of less-than-ideal colors? That's okay. (There is always the next shopping season!) Now that you know what looks best on you, you'll never turn back.

TAKING YOUR ELEMENTS OF STYLE INTO THE CLOSET

for the perfect wardrobe

What a ride! Can you name the three elements of style without looking?[31] Can you name YOUR three elements of style without looking?[32]

I take each one of my clients through the process above and then I turn to her closet. This is exactly where you need to be right now: open that closet (and drawers and under-bed storage . . . and check the floor and the laundry room) and pull out everything you own. (Clean the closet with a soapy sponge while you are at it.) Place everything into the full light of day (on your bed or on rolling racks around the room).

Turn to the sheet on the next page. You'll use this sheet to analyze your current wardrobe and then design your next, fabulous one.

Set aside a few hours for this chore. You'll need a fresh head and a full-length mirror. Good luck!

----

[31] The three "Elements of Style" are fashion personality, proportion in your silhouette, and color palette.

[32] Your three "Elements of Style" are those three terms you determined for yourself so far in this chapter.

CLOSET LOG

Date: ....

Focus Wardrobe: *Personal Casual, School, Business Casual, Dressy*

Season: *Winter, Summer, Transitional*

My Stats:

I am a ....
                    (*my approach*)   (*my muse*)

My natural volume is mostly at my ....

My color palette is ....

This season, the look I'd like could be called:

....

....

1. Check bottoms (trousers and skirts):

___ *The item is pleasing to me.*

___ *The item fits.*

___ *The item gives my overall shape the illusion of proportion.*

___ *The color of the item doesn't cause problems for coordinating a wardrobe.*

___ *The item is in good shape.*

___ *The item sends the message I want to send.*

2. Check tops and dresses:

___ *The item expresses my personality*

___ *The item fits.*

___ *The item gives my overall shape the illusion of proportion.*

___ *The color of the item is flattering to my skin tone.*

___ *The item is in good condition.*

___ *The item sends the message I want to send.*

___ *I have the right bra to wear this top properly.*

3. Check bags, shoes, and jewelry:

___ *The item expresses my personality.*

___ *The item works with the things I own.*

___ *The item is in good condition.*

___ *The item sends the message I want to send.*

I've shopped in my closet and I've found the following fabulous items: (Alternative record: photograph the items in possible coordinated combinations)

I need the following items to finish this wardrobe:

1. .... I budget $ ....

Ideas on where to find it: ....

....

....

2. .... I budget $ ....

Ideas on where to find it: ....

....

....

3. .... I budget $ ....

Ideas on where to find it: ....

....

....

4. .... I budget $ ....

Ideas on where to find it: ....

....

....

5. .... I budget $ ....

Ideas on where to find it: ....

....

....

6. .... I budget $ ....

Ideas on where to find it: ....

....

....

Total amount budgeted: $ ....

HOW TO SHOP LIKE A PRO

Gone are the days when you could easily invest in a few high-quality items, mix and match them for years to come, and not have to change out the clothing unless the weather had changed. This is because we now live in the age of "Fast Fashion."

Fast fashion is the current model for the production and consumption of clothing, and it begins with a producer's sourcing of materials (cotton, leather, etc.), design, manufacturing, distribution, consumption (that's what *we* do), and disposal (we do that too). Traditionally, fashion operated on cycles, which lasted for months between "seasons," but now these cycles are squished together and running "faster," averaging weeks or even days between new arrivals of inventory at any one shopping venue. It might sound truly modern (and it *is* convenient) but there is a whole host of negative consequences that arise from our insatiable desire to fill our closets so often—and so cheaply.[33]

It's a common stereotype that all women like to shop. I think that's a pretty shaky assumption because I know so many women who hate shopping. Whether or not we like to shop, most of us develop some sort of strategy for getting clothes. When I was a full-time college student with no money, I found clothing like treasures in a hunt amidst Goodwill, Amvets, New to You Consignment, and Maryanne's. (Honestly, there were times when I used pocket change.) I had to browse these places regularly, sometimes scoring nothing, sometimes only one article of clothing. The beauty of this method was that over time, I'd have a charming and creative wardrobe that served my needs well.

When I finally began to work full-time, money was still tight, but I could step it up a bit with visits to department stores for things like woolen skirts and higher quality shoes. Those days, I worked with a mental formula for shopping: neutral, high-quality bottoms + cheaper tops + only the very best shoes = presentable work wardrobe.

The following are the three major types of shopping strategies. Which one do you use?

....

33 There is now certainly much more awareness of the dangers of fast fashion than even a few years ago. One resource that has helped is the book *Overdressed: The Shockingly High Cost of Cheap Fashion* by Elizabeth L. Cline.

SHOPPING STRATEGY	CHARACTERISTICS	COMES NATURALLY TO	SUITED BEST FOR
Eclectic	Like an art collector, you regularly gather pieces from just about anywhere (secondhand, offbeat, regular retail) to build up some sort of workable wardrobe.	The **Dreamer, Fashion Plate** or any combination which includes either of these.	Anyone who can regularly visit stores; anyone short on cash; students or professionals who have time to shop regularly.
Formulaic	Like an engineer or an architect, you plan out pieces according to a formula that works for you. (Or, at least you are searching for the perfect formula.)	The **Athlete, Girl Next Door, Lady,** or **Diva** or any combination which includes any of these.	Anyone who can get to stores several times a year; anyone with at least *some* cash for fashion; students or full-time professionals with a moderate amount of time to shop.
Executive	Like an executive, you have a grand plan and you execute it on a schedule only using your most reliable "suppliers." You use this shopping strategy when you stick with the grand plan.	The **Dreamer, Lady, Fashion Plate** or **Diva**	Anyone, especially someone who has difficulty finding time to shop; anyone with a large budget for fashion (but not impossible for those who have limited funds); professionals with a high-profile position.

Answer: *I am a/an* .... *shopper!*

THERE'S A NAME FOR THAT?

Did you know that there was a name for the thing you sometimes do unconsciously? (Or, maybe not so unconsciously?) For shopping, it's a huge help to be able to identify patterns in your behavior so that you can improve your strategy. Check below for how to be the best *eclectic*, *formulaic*, or *executive shopper* you can be!

Tips for the Eclectic Shopper

- Develop a budget for your wardrobe. Before you go shopping, shop your closet first to decide what clothes you need, and then come up with a reasonable amount of money to spend on new clothes. If you use the planning guide in this chapter, you'll stretch your money further.

- An eclectic approach is a great one if you have the time. You could end up burning through gas money if you're going out of your way to hit your favorite places. Combine trips so you can cover a few venues at a time.

- Allocate more money to the items that need to work the most for you. If you travel from one place to another on any given day, ensure that your bag is made of high quality and durable material. If those places are far from one another, you'll need to get better shoes too. Decide where the money goes.

- Before you shop, write out your master plan to figure out which tops go with which bottoms, etc.

- While in a thrift or consignment shop, try on the item. Do not purchase the item if it doesn't fit or if it's stained. If it is damaged beyond repair, don't buy it.

- Once you have the goods, record how the items all go together with your camera. Post the photos so you can see them every morning.

- Most secondhand venues do not allow returns, so "buyer beware." Most regular retailers will accept returns, so be sure not to lose the receipt or clip off the tags prematurely.

Tips for the Formulaic Shopper

- Base your formula on what has worked for you in the past. Possible formulas include:
    1. *3 Dark neutral bottoms + many colorful tops + many cheap fun shoes + really great bag = a mix and match wardrobe of school clothes.*
    2. Or, *4 skirts of different styles and colors + 4 dark neutral color t-shirts + 2 pairs of sandals + 2 bags = a mix and match summer vacation wardrobe*

- Yes, a total of eight items works like the number turned on its side: infinity!

- Allocate more money to the items that need to work the most for you. If you travel from one place to another on any given day, ensure that your bag is made of high quality and durable material. If those places are far from one another, you'll need to get better shoes too. Decide where the money goes.

- Before you shop, write out your master plan to figure out which tops go with which bottoms, etc.

- Be flexible with your formula. If you can't find a "dark brown pencil skirt with a side slit," change the plan to something comparable or you'll be spending an inordinate amount of time shopping.

- Once you have the goods, record how the items all go together with your camera. Post the photos so you can see them every morning.

- Keep receipts and experience notes on your formula.

Tips for the Executive Shopper

- Maybe you're new to this idea, so do a little homework first. Preview department stores and boutiques (without your wallet) to get an idea of styles, who has what, and what inspires you. Get an idea on cost as well.

- Create a budget for your wardrobe.

- If feasible, outsource your planning and shopping by hiring a wardrobe consultant or stylist. Include the price for this service in your budget.

- Write out your grand plan. Will this wardrobe consist of suits or suit-like pieces? Is this a business-casual wardrobe? Will you have several wardrobes: business, business casual, and personal casual? (See page for a template on a starter wardrobe for work.)

- Shop in your closet for any items that will fit nicely into your grand plan.

- Put your money into the hardest working items: skirts, trousers, bag, and shoes.

- You can buy sets (skirt/blouse/jacket) but don't buy second or third versions of any particular item in any set. Rather, use items across sets to get the most out of a single item.

- Keep receipts and experience notes on your purchases.

CHAPTER 5

Leaving My Mark

Media Literacy

Catherine Morland has an overactive imagination from scrolling through conspiracy theory sites and watching cop shows. Recently, however, she read a few social media posts from her friend Tilney, which made Catherine wonder if her friend was up to some illegal activity. Catherine read, "I've got the real deal here . . . come and get it!" "I guarantee a quick fix," and "We had such a trip! It's lit . . . I'm addicted!"

Catherine was genuinely worried about her friend, but instead of asking Tilney directly, Catherine took up a call to action via a post online:

"Hi everybody . . . just want to see who can help with Tilney. She's dealing drugs so we gotta do something!"

You know where I'm headed with this right? After a lot of commotion (yelling, crying, laughing, etc.), Catherine came to find out that the "real deal" in question was actually a therapeutic scented hand cream sold only through home shows. Poor Catherine! She can apologize all she wants, but the message containing the name "Tilney" connected to the words "dealing drugs" is floating around in cyberspace for ever and beyond. Poor Tilney! She has a lot of impossible cleaning up to do.

DON'T LET BAD GO VIRAL

Catherine's case might be extreme, but how many times have you misread an online post, an email, a text, or even a handwritten note? A misinterpretation of any kind of communication—especially a written one—can have very stubborn effects and may damage even the best of relationships.

But it's a two-way street: Catherine is at fault for misreading a post, but Tilney is at fault as well. With a little more care, she could have averted the danger of misinterpretation by using the word "lotion" or "cream" or the brand name of the product in her posts. As with many messages in a world full of "clutter," the messenger may purposely use enticing or provocative language to get attention. Tilney may have been employing a basic marketing strategy and have known exactly what she was doing.

There's a good guide for both ends or roles in any written communication: a guide for the *sender* and a guide for the *receiver*.

1. **Sender:** Use *clear* language that is appropriate for the receiver or any audience.

2. **Receiver:** Know first that you are the intended receiver, evaluate the source of the message, and, if you have a negative emotional

reaction, place the information into any possible context of time constraints and media limitations (i.e., a message's intent or tone is constrained without the corresponding vocal tone, body language, and facial expressions that the spoken word carries). In other words, a strong reaction to a letter, text, post, or email, should always be tempered by the *benefit of the doubt.*

YOU SOUND LIKE MY ENGLISH TEACHER

Why thanks. I'll never sound like your math teacher, I can tell you that.

Since this book is primarily about your own communication as the "sender," we'll begin with that first rule. However, we'll also eventually get to the second guideline for the "receiver" because knowledge of the nature of reception will help you to become a more thoughtful sender.

AN ANCIENT THING CALLED PAPER

and it comes in handy

I don't believe that paper-and-pen correspondence will ever go away. People who predict that physical correspondence will vanish tend to be surrounded by cool technology and lots of electricity. Just watch a toddler with a pen. He'll scribble on paper, the walls, and even his own body. It's an urge, both psychological and tactile, and for naturally developing human beings it continues well into adulthood.

The urge might be satisfied with just a few scrawls for some, but for others, seeing personality and love in the curls of a "s" or a "q" or the beauty of a whole word well-formed is the only way to true, written expression. I'd never take away a laptop for a term paper or an online application for a job, but when a relationship is intimate, it demands an intimate kind of correspondence, a hand-crafted product. I would hope that I'd never leave a typed "good luck" note for a child of mine or a printed love letter for my husband. (But don't reject a love letter just because it's come from a printer. I wouldn't be able to read any of my husband's messages if he didn't type them out.)

What deserves this kind of attention? Consider creating hand-written notes, cards, or letters for the following:

1. Congratulations for a job well done.

2. Sympathy for the loss of a loved one.

3. Thank-you for a gift or a kindness.

4. An invitation to a small gathering.

5. A cheerful letter for down-cast spirits.

6. A love letter.

Antique valentine 1909

Aa Bb Cc Dd Ee
Ff Gg Hh Ii Jj Kk
Ll Mm Nn Oo Pp
Qq Rr Ss Tt Uu
Vv Ww Xx Yy Zz
1234567890
! # $ % & ' ( ) * , - . /

WHEN TO PUT ON YOUR BEST CURSIVE

Once you develop an elegant "hand," you'll want to use it for everything. As you know, however, there is a place for cursive and handwritten correspondences, and then there is the absolute necessity for sending something electronically or having it come through the printer. That's one difference between *informal* and *formal* writing.

Informal writing, which includes cards, letters, or even jottings on post-it notes are intended for friends and family for non-business purposes. (Unfortunately, life may bring business purposes for writing to friends and family one day.) There are rules for informal correspondence:

- Write legibly (that means *clearly*). And write legibly on the envelope too.

- Address it at the top of the actual correspondence: write the name of its intended recipient, followed by a comma. (Even if it's to your little brother.)

- Date it. Just get into the habit of writing the date somewhere toward the top of the note. (Life gets easier when you date absolutely everything.)

- Sign it. You'll probably sign it with just your first name, but that's better than setting up a mystery for someone to solve.

Fitzwilliam Darcy
1813 Pemberly Place
Netherfield, VA 22152

Ms. Lizzy Bennet
1234 Longbourn Lane
Netherfield, VA 22152

DIY: Make your own card-sending system

Written thank-you cards and notes are still as popular as ever. My system of sending thank-you notes and sympathy cards had always been dangerously dependent on actually having a supply of cards, envelopes, and stamps right in front of me within easy reach from a sitting position at my desk. (Now that I use my laptop for everything, bending, reaching, or walking over to my supply shelf seems to be so much work!)

Usually, I'd run out of cards fairly quickly. I always had envelopes (often the wrong size, of course) and a ton of stamps, but then I wouldn't have anything on which to write the actual note besides printer paper or post-it notes, and that has a way of killing the project all together.

Recently, I've made a kit so that I'll never again drop the ball again. Here's how you can do it:

- Find an old briefcase, small "makeup" suitcase, or beautiful box. Whatever you choose must be beautiful to you.

- Load it up with the stamps, blank notecards of varying designs, envelopes, and black pens.

- If you're not good about keeping a digital list of contacts, print off your contacts list with addresses and store it in there as well. Be sure to include the names and addresses of older relatives, especially your grandparents and friends who never use email or social media, and most especially people who often give you a birthday or holiday gift.

- Visit a craft supply store to get blank cards and corresponding envelopes. You can usually find them in bulk.

- Set up a system of your own DIY cards. You can cover your cards with various artistic photographs (a bird, a sunset, the façade of your favorite place), your own drawings or calligraphy, your version of your monogram, or you can decoupage to create unique covers. I decoupage from used wrapping paper, old cards, or even ribbons and buttons. I've created about three cards that way. (I prefer to use photos.)
- Keep the entire kit close to where you like to work.

DIGITAL TRAILS

Much of our correspondence is now online or digital. In fact, the average person is leaving a trail of more personal information than ever before because of the relative ease of computers and cell phones. Technology is wonderfully useful, but we must use it responsibly because, once online, a correspondence never completely disappears. It lives forever in the digital realm even if the original source is deleted. Now that's a sober thought when you think of who could read it: a prospective boss or mentor; unmet friends; a future husband, children, or even grandchildren.

This evidence of your existence works like a trail that leads back to your character. Is the trail worthy of you? No matter what device you use, try to stick to these rules:

1. Never trash talk. Don't use loaded language (like the way a gun or diaper is loaded) and never repeat a negative story about another person—even if it's true.

2. Never use foul language or obscenity, even in a private email and especially in social media. Apply this rule even to foul language that seems to be going mainstream.

3. Unless texting a close friend, capitalize letters where they need to be capitalized, spell correctly, and use punctuation.

4. Never post an inappropriate image or an image that casts another person in a bad light. Never post a less-than-attractive photo of someone else. Also, never tag someone without his or her permission. (Always consider what you might think of someone posting a less-than-admirable photo or post about you: "do to others whatever you would have them do to you."[34])

5. If angry, even justifiably so, give yourself time to cool off a little. Then, speak to the person face to face. If that's impossible, write a draft of what you want to say, check it over, then perfect it so that it reads as logically and objectively as possible before sending it electronically.

6. Rather than whole sentences or phrases, capitalize only single words for emphasis and reduce the number of times you use exclamation points to only short, one- or two-word exclamations. (I can't stand too many exclamation points! It's so annoying!!) See what I mean?

7. Use the words "Awesome!" or "Amazing!" or "LOVE" sparingly. Using such words too often can make you seem insincere.

....

[34] Mt 7:12, NABRE. This is such a practical guideline for getting along that it's called *The Golden Rule*. We'll discuss it again in the last chapter.

8. Never forward other people's contact information without permission or at least serious purpose. Be sure to bcc email addresses for emails sent to many people.

9. Never repeat gossip. That's gossip.

10. Never write assumptions or make connections of which you have no firsthand knowledge.

Your chosen method of communication is determined by where the communication began. So, if someone invites you to a party with an email message, answer back with an email message. If an invitation says to RSVP by a certain date by calling a certain phone number, call that phone number by that certain date.

You can probably categorize the people you know by how you communicate with them. Your best friend only texts you (hopefully, you also still see her in person!); Aunt Alice only writes you letters; your study partners email you. The method they choose is your cue for which method to choose for a response. Sometimes, obviously, you may be the initiator as in the situations below. (The gray section is for communicating with more than one person, and the white section is for communicating with one person only.)

	IN PERSON	HANDWRIT-TEN LETTER	TELEPHONE CALL	EMAIL / SOCIAL NET-WORKING	TEXTING
You want to invite a small group of your best friends out for something special.	What are the chances that everyone would be in one place for your invitation?	Nice touch if you want to be indie about it. The paper invitation is how this has been done for hundreds of years.	Pretty labor-intensive so it's not very practical.	Send an email or a message to your *select* group (rather than a general post), but the response time among everyone will vary. (An email can easily include a map, which may be helpful for your guests.) These methods are best for dates far off in the future.	Most efficient method, but don't forget the details of place, time, and cost. Texting is best for upcoming times (like tonight or tomorrow).
You want to announce great news to all your friends.	With a bull-horn maybe.	Get out the heating pad for writer's cramp.	An effective and personalized way, but it could become labor-intensive.	A social media post allows for this, but be careful not to give away too many personal details online.	Quick and easy, but feedback may not be as fulfilling.
You want to announce bad news to all your friends and family.	No bullhorn here. Maybe take aside friends one by one if possible.	Maybe to your closest friends and family but this is no longer the expected method.	Good for a select number of close friends.	An email or social network message is efficient and can include the necessary details. Don't post it as your status unless connections are expecting an update on previous news.	Only if this is how you usually communicate with them.

	IN PERSON	HANDWRIT-TEN LETTER	TELEPHONE CALL	EMAIL / SOCIAL NET-WORKING	TEXTING
You need to break very bad news to a single friend or family member.	Most definitely. Make the time to do it.	This might work, unless it would be really weird for you to do it.	Only as a backup if you can't get to him or her in person.	Avoid doing this.	Never.
You need to break up with your boyfriend.	Unless there are extenuating circumstances, in person is the best way.	This traditional way is called a "Dear John" letter and is a good back-up.	Another good back-up.	Avoid using anything online. And don't post your break-up for others to see. That's tacky.	Only if something has gone really wrong with the relationship.
You want to ask advice from someone you respect.	Nothing beats this method.	It's hard to get across the finer points unless you are both very adept with letters.	This is a nice alternative to an in-person discussion.	Only through messaging. Much weaker than the telephone. Best to avoid it.	Use this to set up an in-person or telephone date.
You'd like to thank someone for a gift.	Thank the person when you see the person. Always.	A genuine thank-you note is the best for everyone, especially Grandma.	Second to the thank-you note. However, if the person you are thanking is lonely, a phone call is a great way to give the gift of time.	Best for small gifts (like getting a ride to something, or being treated to coffee). A thank-you card is best for actual presents.	Same as online thanking.

	IN PERSON	HANDWRIT-TEN LETTER	TELEPHONE CALL	EMAIL / SOCIAL NET-WORKING	TEXTING
You would like to apologize to someone.	You ought to apologize in person unless it is impossible for you to see the person physically.	A letter makes the apology formal and/or intimate and is usually unnecessary. (I might do it with my husband.)	Second to the in-person apology because the listener can still hear the sincerity in your voice.	A distant third to the in-person method, but it's better than nothing.	Only if you are apologizing for a small matter or something related to a text conversation. For anything more than trivial, follow up with in-person apology.
You want to ask for something (a favor or an item to borrow).	This is the best way if the favor is very involved or complicated.	If you are asking for a very small item, you could drop a quick note.	Second to the in-person request because you have more of an opportunity to explain your request.	Use only for small things or for favors that don't need much explanation.	Use for quick and small things or favors that don't need much explanation.
You want to inquire into the possibility of being hired by a certain business.	Show up but be prepared to return in the future or be given an email address.	Write a letter in business form (a cover letter) to a very large company. Include your resume.	Call the company only if you have the number of a live contact. Then prepare to be told to apply online.	Use the email address you were instructed to use and don't cc anyone else (unless instructed to.) Also, don't brag about doing it on your social networking account.	I can't imagine how texting would work without a prior relationship with someone in the business. Even then, an email is better.

	IN PERSON	HANDWRIT-TEN LETTER	TELEPHONE CALL	EMAIL / SOCIAL NET-WORKING	TEXTING
You need to express your disapproval (maybe even anger) to someone.	Sleep on it first, then see the person face to face.	This is a nice way to gather your thoughts, but do this only if you know you'll lose your temper (or chicken out) in person.	Sleep on it first, try to get a face-to-face meeting, then use a phone call as an alternative if meeting in person is impossible.	Avoid emails or messages. Do not vent about your disapproval anywhere online.	Please no. (That is unless it's an emergency because she is about to do something re-grettable and you know he or she would respond to a text.)

THE GOOD EMAIL

won't let you down

Messages that can move around the world at the speed of light are here to stay. After all, it's a pretty awesome miracle to know that you've sent your message across the world in seconds. What will change is how the technology looks and feels. In the work world, formal writing is always the norm, and so far, email is the domi-nant method for electronic communication because it lends itself so well to clarity and formality.

Below are some basic guidelines for managing your email professionally.

1. Decide if an email is the most appropriate method for what you are trying to communicate. It might not be. You may need to pick up the phone or see your recipient in person.

2. Use the appropriate email address for the recipient. If he's told you not to use his work email address, don't.

3. Let your subject line reflect the contents of the email. Don't leave the subject line blank or vague and don't use sarcasm in your subject line.

4. Be as brief as possible. Use several short paragraphs. If you need to write more than this, pick up the phone or see the recipient in person.

5. Don't bcc to another "secret" person. I mean, really. Don't.

6. Be careful with "reply all" or long strings of email addresses in the "to:" line. Place email addresses in the bcc line if it's a group of people who don't know each other so that no one can see others' email addresses.

7. Respond to "e-stabbing" by taking the high road: don't stab back.

8. Use conventional English. Spell correctly, use uppercase and lowercase letters appropriately, and use exclamation points sparingly.

9. Begin with *Dear So and So*, and end with your name for any new email thread.

10. Keep your signature section succinct and reflective of who you are. Don't load it up with random quotes or huge images.

Find the error

Ready to apply your new knowledge to a real-world email? Read the email below and find features that may be problematic.[35]

My Email
Abigail Action, BigBoss@Actionaccount.com

INBOX
Re: problems
From: Penelope@Actionaccount.com
CC: otherminions@Actionaccount.com

I am so sick of the mess around the office! PEOPLE ARE TOTALLY DISGUSTING! They leave crumbs on the staff lunch table and spill coffee on the tile floor in the lobby. This kind of environment is very hard to work in and I would very much appreciate it if you would speak to the whole staff about it. I would especially like to complain about Mike Messers and Kathy Krumbly as they seem to be the ones standing near the scene of every crime. (I admit I have never actually seen them make a mess, but I know they are.)

-P
Penelope Perspicacious
Accountant, Action Accounting
"Money is the best deodorant." Liz Taylor

---

[35] Answer key: This email shouldn't have been sent in the first place. However, if Penelope is in a position to admonish her coworkers, she should fix the following: 1. Use a more precise subject title such as *Office Environment*, or the friendly, *Let's Work Together to Keep Our Space Clean*. 2. Begin with *Acton Team Members* or *Dear Coworkers*. 3. Delete "I am so sick" and instead begin with a positive reminder or observation. 3. Delete all exclamation points. 4. Delete the entire sentence that is all uppercase. (The caps and the sentence itself are both unprofessional and uncharitable.) 5. Don't mention any names or accuse anyone in writing unless it is an official and confidential human resource document. 6. Delete the "-P." 7. Delete the quote. If a quote must be added, it should be professional-grade, non-offensive, and a positive reflection of the sender. 8. Delete the image. Only use the corporate logo or any required image in company emails.

DO YOU HAVE A THING AGAINST COMPLETE WORDS AND PHRASES?

Why no, LOL!

Supposing I began to write like this: HTF HRU? SWG 2 a COC?

You'd just scratch your head, right? You'd think, "I guess I should know what that means."

Then, you found your friend responding back to me with: HTYS! Yes! I luv a GCOC!![36]

You'd say to yourself, "Oh, that's just some sort of inside joke. I don't care about that."

Yes, you might not care, but you also wouldn't be sure what it is you don't care about. A moment later, you feel kind of left out, don't you? Anyone gets this same feeling when she simply doesn't understand what's been said, like when she gets to a party late, arrives halfway through a lecture, or stumbles through a foreign language. Similarly, written words that make no sense can leave a feeling of disconnection and isolation.

Written language is OBM ("one big miracle." Sorry, I couldn't resist.) It is a way to extend ourselves to facilitate understanding.

But the operative word is *understanding*. Written language must follow certain agreed-upon conventions so that ideas that are "encoded" into symbols on paper may be "decoded" by the reader. This understanding is the reasoning behind your English teacher's insistence upon using conventions for writing. When your writing

---

[36] The first line is "Hi there friend, how are you? Suppose we go to a class on communication." The second line is "Hi there yourself! Yes! I love a good class on communication."

is poor, you not only garble the message, but you also communicate that your writing skills are substandard. You might know the rules and you might even assume that your reader knows you know the rules. But once you choose to ignore the rules, your knowledge of them is no longer evident to the reader and she may guess that you don't know the rules after all!

Below is a description of six things to avoid in your personal, professional, and academic writing. It begins with tips on tone because even the best technically written pieces might be ignored by your reader if the tone is condescending, frivolous, or irritating.

Six persistent pitfalls in writing

1. **Pretension.** If you made it through any grade of high school, you've probably learned how to write under pressure in one night, maybe hours before a paper was due. If you've taken college preparatory classes, you also may have supposed that lots of "smart" words will make it look like you never crammed at all. Well, it doesn't always work:

   Pretentious: *I intend to utilize the tools.*

   Better: *I plan to use the tools.*

   Best: *I'll use the tools.*

   Use plain English even when you are writing for a formal audience. Aim to write with active verbs, precision, and brevity.

2. **Wordiness.** This is related to sounding pretentious, but it stands alone as an issue.

   Wordy: *It is extremely critical to preserve our precious and very important forests or we will suffer miserably and abominably.*

Just Right: *Preserving our forests is critical for our survival.*

Not only is the thesis lost in that first sentence, but the author sounds pretentious.

3. **Inconsistency.** The most common kind of inconsistency is when the subject and verb disagree in number.

   Inconsistent: *The group of students are ready to begin the exam.*

   Just Right: *The group of students is ready to begin the exam.*

   Better: *The students are ready to begin the exam.*

   Another kind of inconsistency happens between a noun and a pronoun:

   Inconsistent: *The student liked to get their books at a good price.*

   Just Right: *The student liked to get his books at a good price.*

4. **Ambiguity**: It could be that a sentence contradicts itself or has a double meaning (officially called *syntactic ambiguity*).

   Inconsistent: *I saw a girl at the party with purple hair.* (I personally have never seen a party with purple hair.)

   Better: *I saw a girl at the party who had purple hair.*

5. **Carelessness.** It happens especially in word choice and spelling: for example, the mix-up with *it's, its, your, you're, their, there,* and *they're.* These are homophones, words that sound the same but are spelled differently. You have to be careful because

spell-checking programs will miss these mistakes.

Careless choice of spelling: *Its you're turn to bring there chairs in.*

Correct: *It's your turn to bring their chairs in.*

6. **Misfired figure of speech**. The most common kind of misfire is the mixed metaphor.

Misfire: *The gaggle of women roared their way into the restaurant.*

Better: *The gaggle of women honked their way into the restaurant.* (Geese don't roar; they honk.)

How do you catch these things? You proofread. Then, you have a competent peer proofread your work as well. This doesn't mean that when you wrap up your writing at midnight, you read it through before printing it off at 12:05 a.m. You sleep on it. The more space between writing and proofing, the better your writing will be. That's why it's good to heed your teacher's advice to start early on any assignment.[37]

Many of you might say, "I write better under pressure!" So do I. To get around that, put some artificial pressure on yourself (realistically, *at least* a few days before a deadline for a small to medium-sized project) and then turn off your car radio, pull out your ear buds, and allow yourself to develop your ideas while you *aren't at the computer.* Brain experts say that the best "aha" moments occur when we aren't engaged in the task itself.

....

[37] The classic "Elements of Style" by William Strunk and E.B. White is still an easy and accessible reference for writing well.

Finally, do two things when you proofread in addition to reading your work silently, looking for errors. First, read your work *aloud* for clarity, understanding, and flow, and then read it backward, word by word, for the word-level errors.

OMT (One More Thing . . .)

When did we begin using terms like LOL or BFF?

We modern people aren't the first people to use letters to stand for words. A poem from the eighteenth century, repeated by Charles C. Bombaugh in the nineteenth century reads, "He says he loves U 2 X S, / U R virtuous and Y's." and "In X L N C U X L / All others in his I's."[38] (Kind of cute, isn't it?)

In the time of your great-grandparents, right around the Great Depression, the United States Government (that's the U.S.A.) began initiatives that were known more by their abbreviations than their full names, in the same way we all know what IRS, FBI, or CIA means today. (By the way, an abbreviation is when letters stand for a word and only the letters are pronounced, like FBI; an acronym is when letters stand for a word and are pronounced as a word, like NASA.)

Then, there are abbreviations that have been around for so long we've forgotten what they mean:

etc.—et cetera, Latin (meaning "and the rest")

i.e.—id est, Latin (meaning "that is")

a.m.—ante meridiem, Latin, (meaning "before noon and after midnight")

---

[38] "He says he loves you to excess, / You are virtuous and wise." "In excellence you excel / All others in his eyes."

p.m.—post meridiem Latin (meaning "after noon and before midnight")

ibid—ibedem, Latin (meaning the "same place"; it's used in bibliographies and footnotes)

RSVP—répondez s'il vous plaît, (from the French for "please respond")

AD or A.D.—Anno Domini (from Latin, "In the Year of Our Lord" as in the "year 1776 AD" or "2013 AD") CE—"Common Era" (from the English alternative for Anno Domini, but meaning the same span of time)

BC or B.C.—"Before Christ" (Designating any year before the time of Christ and therefore before the start of AD, as in the year 336 BC)

BCE—"Before the Common Era" (from the English alternative for Before Christ, but meaning the same span of time)

Newer abbreviations include:

A.A.—Associate of Arts (a two-year college degree certificate)

B.A.—Bachelor of Arts

BCC—blind carbon-copy (on an email)

B.S.—Bachelor of Science

CC—carbon-copy (on an email)

CPA—Certified Public Accountant

JPEG—Joint Photographics Experts Group—the people who invented .jpg.

LCD—Liquid Crystal Display

LED—Light Emitting Diode

M.D. —Doctor of Medicine, from the Latin Medicinae Doctor

MD—is the great state of Maryland. The United States Postal Service (USPS) codes are appropriate in just about every situation. These abbreviations for states are capital letters with no periods between them.

M.B.A.—Master of Business Administration

Ph.D.—Doctor of Philosophy

YMCA—an organization whose full name is Young Men's Christian Association

YWCA—Yup, there's a Young Women's Christian Association too.

Crazy English (and what's up with the word "gaggle?")
You may have been corrected from saying "I could care less" to the proper phrase "I *couldn't* care less," or "one in the same" to the correct wording, "One *and* the same." Then, there is the crazy "all intensive purposes," which should be said "all *intents and* purposes." (These mistakes are called "eggcorns.")[39] When you take a moment to think about it, you realize that if you meant the expression literally, it would be contradictory and silly.

---

[39] The term "eggcorn" was coined by the linguist Geoffrey Pullum in September 2003 on a website. It was a nod to a subject's substitution of "acorn" with "eggcorn." These mistakes are especially egregious when written out.

But then, you're told not to take many other phrases literally. Think about the last time someone pleaded with you to explain yourself: *"Just tell me and don't beat around the bush!"*

This linguistic phenomenon is called an *idiomatic expression*, and while it may trip up English language learners, its use tends to become second nature for fluent speakers. I like to think of idioms as a spice rack of tasty zingers that can flavor our language in a way that makes the meal of everyday talk, a rowdy banquet in celebration of life! (Yes, that's a metaphor, and I didn't mix anything up!)

Below are a few idioms that are often misused:

- *Actions speak louder than words* means that what people do is more believable than what they say. It's usually a reminder or a call to action.

- *Add insult to injury* means to make a bad situation worse so that it's a second stage in a chain of negative events.

- *A perfect storm* means the worst possible situation. (It's not used for an ordinary or normally expected event.)

- *Better late than never* means that it's better to arrive late than not at all.

- *Cut the mustard* means to do a good job.

- *Don't beat a dead horse* means to move on from a subject because it has been thoroughly covered.

- *Get wind of [something]* means to hear of something secret.

- *Make hay while the sun shines* means to take advantage of a *good* situation. (It's not used in reference to a bad situation.)

- *The elephant in the room* means the big issue that everyone knows about but no one wants to talk about.
- *Waste not, want not* means that if you don't waste things, you'll always have enough.
- *Wrap your head around [something]* means to try to understand something complicated.[40]

Remember that word *gaggle* from the example of a misfired figure of speech? The word "gaggle" is a collective noun (specifically a *term of venery*, or a name for a group of animals), which dates back to the Middle Ages when the hunting culture was developing in England. It seems the medieval English liked to be accurate about what kind of animal they were hunting. But they had fun using these animal terms to refer in a tongue-in-cheek way to a *gaggle of women* or a *sentence of judges*. A light-hearted application of a term of venery to a group of people can make writing more interesting to read.

My seventh grade English teacher, Sister Margaret, had us memorize some of fun ones:

- a colony of ants
- a sleuth of bears
- a flock of birds
- a herd of buffalo
- a clutter of cats
- a brood of chickens
- a pack of dogs

[40] A great resource for the history of idioms is *The American Heritage Dictionary of Idioms.*

- a school of dolphins
- a raft of ducks
- a troop of foxes
- an army of frogs
- a gaggle of geese
- a team of horses
- a mob of kangaroos
- a pride of lions
- a parliament of owls
- a flock of sheep
- a streak of tigers
- a cohort of zebra

I UNDERSTAND YOU CLEARLY

Let's return to the second rule for written communication:

Receiver: Be sure that you are the intended receiver, evaluate the source of the message, and, if you have a negative emotional reaction, place the information into any possible context of time constraints and media limitations (i.e., a message's intent or tone is constrained without the corresponding vocal tone, body language, and facial expressions that the spoken word carries.) In other words, a strong reaction to a letter, text, post, or email, should always be tempered by the *benefit of the doubt.*[41]

There's *three* rules packed into that one, so let's break it down:

1. Know that you are the intended receiver. The author of a message may have assumed that the audience has prior knowledge or familiarity with the subject matter. In fact, the person may not have meant the message for you at all. (Think about how you came upon the message. Are you a legitimate receiver?) This is when you say to yourself, "There must be more to the story."

2. Evaluate the source of the message. If the message is making untrue statements or misguided opinions, address those items, but do not attack the writer. (That's called an *ad hominem* attack.) Place effort in your rebuttal only to the extent that it will help anyone in the long run.

3. If you have a strong reaction, especially a negative one, consider the possibility that the writer may have written very quickly, not known the rules of clear English (like you do now), or had a completely different tone in mind while writing. Generally, people don't intend to offend others in written communications, but when they do, their message will often leave very little room for doubt! So, if there is room for doubt, give them the benefit of it!

....

[41] "Giving the benefit of the doubt" is another idiom, which goes back probably to the early 1800s, based on the idea that in court one must give the verdict of "not guilty" where evidence is weak. In serious situations, you should only give the benefit of the doubt when you suspect a person really deserves it.

Let's visit the beginning of what eventually becomes a well-known love story:

Lizzie Bennet always believed that she was a reasonable and fair-minded woman. So, she was taken aback when she came to realize that she loathed a schoolmate she barely knew. First, the guy had a reputation for being a snob and his profile page only seemed to prove it. In person, he used words like "condescend" and "affinity" (oh please!), hung out with snobs, and provided terse comments to people's innocent online posts. The handful of texts she had exchanged with him about a class project were brief (on his part), and he never acknowledged her mentioning the names of mutual friends. She had to just assume that the guy was hopelessly stuck-up and would never become a true friend.

Well, with that attitude, the two won't ever become friends, that's for sure. But was Lizzie correct in assuming the guy was a hopeless snob?

Based on the information we have, it's hard to say. *We only have Lizzie's point of view.* She is prejudiced against her schoolmate so much that anything he says or writes will be seen as snobbery.

Also, the remote and brief nature of their encounters doesn't help Lizzie understand her schoolmate better. When there is correspondence, Lizzie sees aloofness where truthfully there might only be shyness or reserve. (Yes, this guy might have a type of pride that is ruining his chances for good relationships. But we aren't discussing him right now.)

Their written communications are making Lizzie's understanding of her schoolmate worse. Shyness may be understood and excused in person, but heaven help the reserved guy who doesn't get with the program online. Short comments, reticence, or even a dry sense of humor can come off as rudeness, snobbery, or meanness when there aren't any contextual cues like body language or facial expressions to indicate otherwise.

How could Lizzie have tempered her natural reactions to what appears to be pride and prejudice? Well, she could read the first chapter of this book, especially the part that explains how each one of us is SUBJECT, worthy of respect because of our God-given value. If she acts on this reality and understands that we can never completely know another person's motives (or true moods, challenges, or limitations), then she would show mercy to him by giving the *benefit of the doubt*. She would resist the temptation to label or stereotype him and instead treat him with fairness and charity.

Imagine how our communications, connections, and ultimately relationships would improve if we lived respect and restraint?

A WORLD-WIDE WEB OF WONDER

or shiny bright objects to distract us

Take a moment to consider everything you have read in the last twenty-four hours: history homework, a set of directions, a recipe, part of an article, a webpage, your map app, road signs, social media posts, a few emails, and a whole bunch of texts.

Oh wait, look back again. Don't forget food and cosmetics labels, company logos, billboards, online banner ads, video ads, cell phone ads, magazine covers, and even the sides of the trucks and buses that pass you on the highway. These messages, unlike your personal correspondences, are one-way, mostly paid-for marketing efforts, which constitute a large portion of your visual landscape.

Now, before you skip ahead to another topic, think about the effects of splitting your attention and energy across a huge array of products, celebrities, intriguing destinations, and ideas. You're being pulled into a million directions so much, that perhaps you've developed coping mechanisms such as attending to only the most provocative, listening to the loudest, watching the biggest, or responding to the most alluring messages in the mix.

If you suddenly feel wanted and valued, that's great. After all, you hold the power as a consumer in a large and sophisticated economy, and brands are vying to tap into the pot of gold known as *Generation Z.* (That's you.)

On the other hand, with so much of our attention, time, and energy consumed by the pursuit of the right brand name style, or the most "relevant" product, or even the socially responsible company, there may not be time to consider yourself as anything other than a consumer.

At a certain point in any semester when I teach fashion marketing, we get to explore an area of knowledge called Self Concept Theory, which works a lot like it sounds: *I have a concept of myself as a person and it drives my self-esteem, my goals, and most of my consumption decisions.* The part of this theory that gives me pause is the idea of the "extended self," which holds that our possessions contribute to our self-identity, and, for that matter, our sense of self-worth.

Now just think about that: if we each have an *actual infinite value* as a person, why would we be inclined to measure this value with the pitiful gauge of material possessions? It's sort of like using a standard twelve-inch ruler to measure the light years between galaxies! If we follow this logic, we'll never get an accurate appraisal of who we are.

The thoughtful consumption of any good, service, or idea involves planning, purchasing, using, and sometimes disposing in a way that stays loyal to who you are and why you are here in this world of ours.

Media literacy
begins with smart consumption

The ideas below may seem far from the skills related to communication, but these attitudes are necessary for skillfully responding to any kind of media message.

1. View your personal items, especially the big ones, as "tools on loan." The "on loan" aspect may inspire you to take care of your stuff (clean, repair, maintain) and immunize you from allowing the loss of something from becoming an overwhelming emotional burden.

2. Attitude #1 will help you to *put people before things*. So, whenever a decision must be made such as, for example, the decision to keep a personal item in pristine condition by keeping it away from others OR loaning the item to someone who can use it, thus risking damage or loss, decide on loaning the item if you know that the person truly needs it for a good purpose.

3. Once you try to live by #1 and #2, you'll also come to realize that shopping will never end in *complete* satisfaction. Often, especially in regard to fashion purchases, people shop out of *self-illusory hedonism*, which is daydreaming about the promises of a purchase. After the purchase is made, the daydreams

never come to reality, and so the shopper begins to daydream about other products to buy. It's a nasty and expensive cycle.[42]

4. Think of your shopping in terms of problem-solving and resist the urge to see any purchase as fulfilling more in your life than solving that one problem or set of problems. And, as in all kinds of problem-solving, search for information on the options for purchase and, as much as possible, try to stay rational.

5. If you live also by #3, then you will naturally depart from the idea that you are what you own. At this level, you can resist getting on the never-ending conveyer belt of acquisition—disposal—acquisition—disposal.

6. Dispose of an item in the least impactful way: reuse it, reinvent it, recycle it, or give it away before letting it settle into a landfill. You should also consider how difficult an item or its packaging is to dispose of before purchasing it.

FOOD FOR THE SOUL

Or, good nutritional information

Hopefully, you are reading more than billboards, texts, or blog posts. Reading thoughtful writing, especially essays and literature, goes beyond the mere acquisition of helpful information or good entertainment; it can be food for the soul. Such works enrich your

---

[42] The idea of *self-illusory hedonism* was first described by the sociologist Collin Campbell, to whom I am very grateful.

thinking, help you to become more empathetic, and can inspire you to grow into a better and more generous person.

Of course, not all reading material is good for the soul. Choosing what to read is a judgment call.[43] It's an important judgement, however, because the writer-reader relationship, especially in fiction, can be so intimate that this relationship may literally change the life of the reader.

Literature's younger sister, cinema, can have the same effects on the viewer. Since we spend at least as much time feeding the soul with movies and television shows as with literature, it's good to have a measuring stick for choosing the best of both:[44]

- *Does the book or movie improve my ability to connect, communicate, and ultimately understand others through its helpful portrayal of the human person?*

- *Does it ignite a passion in me to do something good or start a project with the real potential of inspiring others to do something good?*

- *Does it inspire me to become a better person so that others can connect, communicate, and ultimately understand me?*

Have you ever felt depressed, anxious, or simply angry after watching or reading something? Sometimes those feelings eventually lead to any one (or all) of the objectives above and can be the

....

[43] Judge what you digest: books, movies, articles, food, medicine, etc.
[44] This list could also be a good measure on the value of what you choose to write.

beginning of the best life changes. But when these feelings remain *only* depression, anxiety, or anger, or lead to any kind of isolation, then watching or reading has become counter-productive. It may have even embittered you or predisposed you to cynicism, negativity, and inaction.

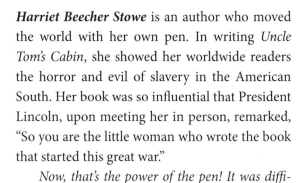

Harriet Beecher Stowe is an author who moved the world with her own pen. In writing *Uncle Tom's Cabin*, she showed her worldwide readers the horror and evil of slavery in the American South. Her book was so influential that President Lincoln, upon meeting her in person, remarked, "So you are the little woman who wrote the book that started this great war."

Now, that's the power of the pen! It was difficult for me to get through the first half of this book because of the intensity of the subject matter. However, a friend of mine encouraged me to finish the book, and I'm so grateful that I did because not only was the story thrilling, it became the inspiration for me to think more deeply on issues regarding human dignity, race, and stereotyping.

JUNK FOOD

And now we arrive at one of the junkiest forms of your reading diet: the news. When your political science teacher recommended that you keep up with current events, she wasn't referring to who on the red carpet was wearing Louboutin heels, or exactly how people died in the latest traffic accident, or even what single food type reduces your chances of catching yellow fever. There might be a time when any of that type of information is needed, but staying informed is more about knowing the basic facts of current events, how they spring from the past, how they affect the present situation, and how they can shape the future. Your teacher wants you to become an informed member of our society, able to advance the public conversation in a thoughtful and positive way.

The problem is that news is a commodity and will be traded around, dressed up, and paraded out to attract consumers' attention. In some cases it's click-bait, and in the worst of cases, someone's intentionally trying to sway your opinion for malicious purposes. Even in the most innocent of binge-surfing, readers may find that after investing a lot of attention, they're left with only the empty feeling that comes from wasting time.

So, judge your information and sources (articles, books, blogs, hearsay) with a checklist like this one:

1. *Do I really need to know this information? Honestly?*

2. *What are the proven facts of the story? How have they been proven? Is it enough proof?*

3. *Is the source credible? Does it have a bias? Will the source benefit in some way from how a particular news item plays out?*

"*What information consumes is rather obvious. It consumes the attention of its recipients. Hence a wealth of information creates a poverty of attention.*" – Herbert Simon, Nobel Prize-winning economist

CHAPTER 6

See What I Mean?

Virtue and Manners

Let's peek at Fanny from Chapter 1 again:

Fanny thought about her interview with her boss and where it could have possibly gone wrong. She thought she'd said all the right things, but obviously (since she didn't get the promotion) she communicated other things in other ways. In the light of a new day, she realized what they were:

- *I was four minutes late to the interview. (What did that say about my work habits?)*

- *I was wearing my "comfy" yoga pants. (What did that say about my attitude and sense of professionalism?)*

- *I was a little distracted when I walked into that interview and I glanced around while my boss spoke. (What did that say about my priorities and respect for my boss?)*

She certainly didn't look like she'd meant what she was saying to her boss. And that's a pity. Proving our words through our actions ensures that our connections and communications lead to real understanding.

In Chapter 3 we discussed the power of a first impression enough to know not to choose "comfy" casual clothing for something as important as an interview for a promotion. But there's more. As we can see, Fanny made mistakes in body language and action, two sorts of mistake that don't happen in only professional settings. They can make a mess in our personal lives as well.

I LEFT MY MANNERS AT MY GRANDMA'S

and it looks like Emma did too:

Emma Woodhouse was so thrilled to host a get-together that she can't figure out how she allowed herself to insult one her guests. She didn't mean to; she just blurted out a biting criticism in a word game that was supposed to show off her wit and cleverness. The guest, who admires Emma for her supposed social graces (and who rarely gets invited to these kinds of things anyway), was truly hurt by the remark because everyone—including some people she had just met—heard it. She also secretly knew it to be true and was embarrassed.

Oh, badly done Emma.

Was the blurt-out just a "mistake" in the way that we like to call anything that turns out unexpectedly a "mistake"? It was more than that: it was a bad move. It was rude. It was mean. But let's not dwell on the negative here. (Emma wouldn't.) The best thing she can do is sincerely apologize to her guest and resolve to be conscious about what she says in the future.

Is the apology necessary because *etiquette* demands it? Well, yes. But there's more. The apology is necessary because *justice* demands it. Emma has wronged her guest and owes her an in-person, face-to-face acknowledgement of her wrongdoing and a request for forgiveness.

Good etiquette or, more broadly speaking, *manners* are rooted in simple, baseline justice. Manners are the road map for right and wrong in social behavior. The source of this justice is the subject of other books and can't be treated here without adding a bunch of chapters.[45]

Civility, etiquette, manners

These three words aren't, after all, interchangeable. There are distinctions:

CIVILITY	ETIQUETTE	MANNERS
The absence of hostility	A code (often written) that can be arbitrary	A code (rarely written) that is not arbitrary
Universally expected	Specific to a culture or subculture	Universally appreciated
Reflects an ability to function among others	Reflects training	Reflects good character

....

[45] I'm not so sure I could write that book, as so many better ones are out there already (like, say, the *New Testament*). The first chapter of this book, however, provides a hint to justice's Source.

If you glance at any popular sources on etiquette, you might get the impression that manners are for getting what you want or moving ahead in business. Well, any etiquette book worth its weight in paper is rooted in the idea that we owe each other respect in the form of common courtesy because of our value as persons. Over-concern for which fork is used on lobster or the difference between a *champagne flute* and a *champagne toasting flute* is way beside the point.

Most of us get that. We seem to be born with the idea that others deserve our respect. (Or, our mothers get the idea into us.) We learn the "Golden Rule," that we should only do to others what we would have them do to us.

Fanny knew she needed to convey respect to her employer but took all the nonverbal communication for granted. Emma, on the other hand, also desired good things, but did the opposite of what Fanny did. She went through all the motions to make her guests feel comfortable but became thoughtless in her verbal communication.

Have you ever had either of those experiences? They aren't pleasant, are they?

The situation gets even bleaker when we are wrong in what we think we are communicating. For example, the fifty-year-old who dresses like she's seventeen might think she's projecting youth, health, and what she thinks is sexiness, but others perceive a shame of age, indiscretion, and lack of good taste.

So, let's take a sampling of actions:

WHAT YOU DO (OR DIDN'T DO):	PROJECTION (WHAT YOU THINK YOU COMMUNICATE):	PERCEPTION (WHAT OTHERS UNDERSTAND FROM YOUR COMMUNICATION):
You are five minutes late to a club meeting.	*I am laid back and flexible about rules.*	The club is not a high priority for you.
You keep a serious and pensive face while being introduced to others.	*I am thoughtful and intelligent.*	You are aloof and maybe even stuck up. You don't seem interested in meeting these new people.
You didn't place your napkin on your lap during dinner.	*I wasn't really thinking at all.*	You are careless, ignorant, or both.

It's a lot to keep track of, isn't it? So, rather than breaking down courtesy (or respect, really) into a list of do's and don'ts, let's examine it for multiple attitudes, often called the ***social graces***, which are rarely ever misconstrued. We just all know grace when we feel it. (Each social grace builds on the preceding one.)

"*How noble and good everyone could be if, every evening before falling asleep, they were to recall to their minds the events of the whole day and consider exactly what has been good and bad. Then without realizing it, you try to improve yourself at the start of each new day; of course, you achieve quite a lot in the course of time. Anyone can do this, it costs nothing and is certainly very helpful. Whoever doesn't know it must learn and find by experience that: 'A quiet conscience makes one strong!'*" —Anne Frank, "Diary of a Young Girl"

SOCIAL GRACE	SOCIAL GRACE
Kindness—the baseline of social graces.	**Fashion**: You've taken care of basic hygiene such as body odor and breath. You're clean. You avoid wearing offensive fashion statements or body art.
	Body Language: You keep the culture's (whichever one you are in) conventional distance from another. You face the person who is speaking to you, acknowledging his or her presence.
	Action: You are punctual and aim to cooperate in making an event a success. You ask after another person: "How are you today?" You allow the other person to answer. You resist voicing judgment and restrain random blurts. You don't cuss. You adjust the volume of your voice to the context (i.e., you don't talk so loudly you hurt a person's hearing). You chew your food (or gum) with your mouth closed and dab your mouth with your napkin when necessary.
Warmth—what makes the world a nice place to live in.	**Fashion**: You avoid pretension in your dress. You bring out your inner warmth with colors and makeup that make your face glow.
	Body Language: You gesture naturally with your hands (palms up rather than down), avoiding arm crossing or finger pointing. You affirm the other's presence with eye contact and occasional (but not excessive) head-nodding to show you are listening. You SMILE even when you don't feel like it.
	Action: You ask after the concerns of others. You follow up on past conversations. You check the needs of others (e.g., "would you like a second cup of coffee?"). You never let on that a guest's innocent actions are an inconvenience for you.

SOCIAL GRACE	SOCIAL GRACE
Discretion—what distinguishes women from little girls.	**Fashion:** You choose the appropriate clothing for the occasion (see Chapter 3). You choose clothing that keeps the focal point on your face.
	Body Language: You sit as a woman by keeping your knees together. You resist emitting loud body noises. You refuse to do things in public that are best left for private time.
	Action: You avoid speaking crudely or giving away too much information or information that's meant to be private.
Inspiration—what can make you a leader.	**Fashion:** Your clothing choices are tasteful and creative and distinguish you from the others.
	Body Language: You stand up straight with your shoulders back. You walk like a person with a purpose (and not like someone with a secret to protect). You sit up in your chair as if you care about the others around you.
	Action: You always greet newcomers and introduce people in your presence; you speak with correct grammar and aim for topics that are interesting to other people besides you.

Learning the above social graces is like becoming fluent in a language. It makes living in the world so much easier!

Pick one: *In which social grace can I improve? How?*

....

....

....

HOW TO GIVE A GREAT JOB INTERVIEW

Break down the event into three phases:

Before the interview demonstrate your ability to prepare . . .

1. Research the business. What are they proud of? What is their current big news?

2. Get accurate directions for the location of the interview or figure out the bus route. (Note that an interview is not necessarily at the place of business.) If possible, drive past the location ahead of time to be sure you know where it is. Know where to park, how much it costs, and whether you pay with cash or a credit card.

3. Figure out appropriate attire for the interview. What are the standards of the profession or the "office culture" of that particular place? Gather together the items for your outfit (top, bottom, shoes, bag, hosiery—yes, hosiery) and ensure that each is cleaned and pressed. (Do this while there is still time to change your clothing plan.)

During the interview communicate your professional attitude and intelligence . . .

1. Arrive about five minutes early to the interview.

2. Greet your interviewer with eye contact, a smile, and a firm handshake. (See page 43)

3. Sit when and where you are indicated to sit.

4. Sit up straight but don't lean back in your chair. Continue to look the interviewer in the eyes while speaking or being spoken to.

5. Answer his or her questions without slang or vulgarity. Live justice in your words by avoiding criticism of past work-related people or events.

6. Part with a "thank you for your time" to the interviewer. Avoid lingering when others are waiting or when your interviewer is trying to go to another activity.

After the interview communicate your gratitude . . .

1. Mail the interviewer a hand-written thank-you note, unless the company specializes in another method of correspondence, in which case, you should use that other method (like a digital messenger or social media company).

2. Provide anything you promised to provide to the interviewer the same (or next) day.

DRESSING FOR SUCCESS

Can begin with just 8 pieces

Whenever anyone provides advice on giving a good interview, she must also discuss the clothing that's required. Fortunately, the items you would choose for a job interview can also work for things like a religious service, a fancy meal, or an interview that's part of a school or college application process. There are times in your life, however, when these events are clustered into a single month or season. That's when it's time to make an investment in yourself by purchasing what I call below "The Eight Piece Starter Wardrobe."

The starter wardrobe (or, usually, the seed of a starter wardrobe) is exactly what I am providing my clients at the *Success In Style* Studio at the Job Corps Campus in Washington, DC. Working with both men and women in our elegant boutique (which the students from the Job Corps built themselves!), I discuss the language of pieces like "authority of the suit jacket," the "polished look of a dress shirt," or the "smaller details" like clean shoes and an understated bag. My clients, in turn, carry a confidence in the message of their fashion right into their job interviews.

THE 8 PIECE STARTER WARDROBE

1 cardigan (in your best color!)

1 blazer in your best dark neutral

1 scoop neck blouse in solid or print

1 "man-tailored" white shirt

This should be your investment piece

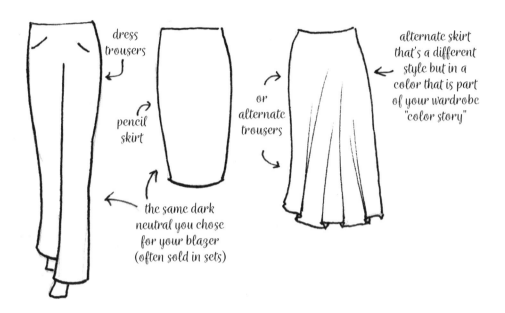

dress trousers

pencil skirt

or alternate trousers

alternate skirt that's a different style but in a color that is part of your wardrobe "color story"

the same dark neutral you chose for your blazer (often sold in sets)

Checklist:
· 2 flesh-toned bras
· hosiery
· flat dress shoes
· black pumps
· well-made tote or satchel
· favorite jewelry and/or fashion scarf

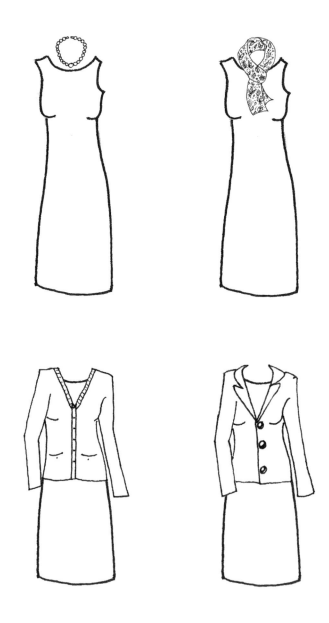

MANNERS AREN'T JUST FOR GRANDMA

The term "etiquette" and the idea of good manners get a bad rap. After all, our culture has spent dozens of years mocking the lifted pinkie or the lobster fork. I don't know about you, but if I thought good manners only involved a lifted pinkie or a lobster fork, I'd mock it too.

But it's so much more than that. George Washington wrote of 101 "Rules of Civility," which began, "Every Action done in Company, ought to be with Some Sign of Respect to those that are Present," and ended with "Labour to keep alive in your Breast that Little Spark of Celestial fire Called Conscience." (No mention of a lobster fork there.) Emily Post left her legacy of etiquette through her reference book on manners, which is now enjoying its eighteenth edition and includes everything from flags on caskets to dealing with angry telephone callers. Any one of us can write to Judith Martin as "Miss Manners" on just about any topic under the sun. Good manners are about people living with one another.

Queen Margaret of Scotland lived in a rough period of time for Western Europe (1045–1093). She was descended from English (Saxon) kings, grew up in Hungary, but became the queen of Scotland when she married King Malcolm Canmore (the same one from Shakespeare's play Macbeth). This King Malcolm III was a bit of a barbarian but he was madly in love with Margaret. She cleaned him up and brought literacy, manners, and civility into his court, perhaps allowing for more peace to *reign in the country, as she showed her husband that endless war-fare was wrong. She is best known for holding off her own break-fast until she personally fed two hundred beggars at the castle.*[46]

CELL PHONES AND THE STONE AGE

I remember my first cell phone. It was the size of a brick and weighed about the same. I loved having others notice me use it because it was just so ahead of its time, and I wanted everyone to know that I could afford both to have a cell phone *and* use it to call people. Imagine that.

You laugh, but don't you think people still do that? People want others to know that they have the latest whatever, or, these days anyway, they want you to know that they are connected to other people who are far more interesting than you or anyone else physically in the room with them. Cave people from the Stone Age, peeking in on a modern family meal, might notice something:

Caveman: Everyone seems to be eating a delicious bit of meat here. That pronged instrument is a brilliant idea! Why didn't I think of it? But wait! something's wrong with this picture . . . I can't quite put my finger on it.

Cavewoman: Oh, I can! There are those black things in front of their faces. Each person doesn't even know that other people are eating with them.

---

[46] Icon of Queen (St.) Margaret by Marice Sariola (www.iconsbymarice.com.au)

Caveman: *Looks like evil spirits are inside those things and everyone is just fine with that.*

Cavewoman: *Yeah, that must be what's happening. I thought modern humans were going to be smarter than us. I might need to go back and adjust my theory on the progress of our intelligence.*

Smart phone management comes down to setting a few personal habits:

1. Set up your cell phone thoughtfully. Choose a screen image that is appropriate for all audiences. Keep the sound setting on vibrate, or choose a low-key, unassuming ring tone.

2. If you don't check your voicemail, don't set it up to receive messages.

3. Do not drive and text.

4. Check your voicemail at least once a day. Try to return calls the same day.

5. Before returning a phone call, check voicemail to see what the person has left as a message. I know of someone who lost an internship because she carelessly called back the prospective manager before she checked the details on the voicemail.

6. Keep your phone conversations private, especially while in public places such as stores, public transportation venues, or waiting in line.

7. Do not use your phone (even to text) while in a theater, meeting, church service, or a shared meal.

8. Keep your phone off the table during a meal. Do not answer it during a meal or date.

9. Do not walk around talking loudly into the phone. (Try to talk ten feet away from other people and with a slightly quieter than regular speaking volume.)

11. Remove your ear device when you are interacting with people who are providing you service. Stop your phone call when you arrive at the cashier, information desk, or any other service person's presence. (Each of those people is a person and deserves your full attention.)

DINING ETIQUETTE

Everyone eats—every animal, every human, no exception. Add to that the fact that the act of eating is a rather base, violent thing to do. You are stabbing things with a pronged instrument, cutting with a knife, sticking stuff into your mouth, mashing the stuff up with your teeth, and swallowing with everyone knowing that the next time the same food makes an appearance, well, you know.

So it's little wonder that eating is the showcase for manners. In fact, we not only have social situations that require the arts involved with dining, but business situations as well. Some interviews may even involve a dining component for the interviewers to observe a candidate's poise, self-control, and capacity for good judgment.

It's important to develop the habits involved with dining etiquette for daily life, rather than relegating them to those rare events like business lunches or interviews. Below is a survey of what you need to know.

Upon Entering . . .

the dining area, take a cue from the host or hostess on where to sit. If a place card indicates your place, obey it. Never trade places or rearrange place cards.

- Seat yourself when the host or hostess indicates that it is time. Once seated, watch the host or hostess place his or her own napkin before placing your own. (Business: Place your napkin in your lap as soon as you sit down.)

- If someone, especially a male, pulls your chair for you, thank him. (Business: Men do not pull chairs for women; men and women need to assist only those who physically need the help. If a man does assist you with your chair, simply nod, rather than correcting him in front of the group.)

- Sit up straight in your chair with your elbows off the table. Phone, keys, bag, papers, and wallet stay off the table and on the floor under your chair or table.

- Speak to the person on your right *and* left if possible and appropriate. Learn names. Repeat them in your greetings.

- If you are someone's guest, then generally he or she is paying for your meal. However, always have a credit card or cash on you in case your host or hostess is a little confused about dining etiquette. If she is not confused, she will probably give cues as to what she feels comfortable paying for. So, for example, she may say that the "beef is delicious." This is a cue that you can order the beef or a dish similar in price.

- If you are a vegetarian or allergic to a certain food, order something you can eat without giving an explanation. Generally, when a dinner is being set up, information concerning diet restraints is communicated.

- Do not order alcohol unless you are of age and your host is drinking it herself. If you choose to have a glass of wine or beer, sip slowly through the meal rather than gulping it before the food comes.

Below is something close to (or maybe exactly) what you will see at your place setting:

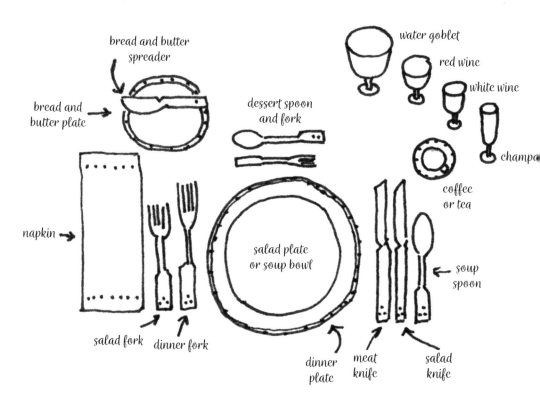

Tips:

1. Remember BMW! (Bread on left, Meal in middle, Water or liquids on right)

2. Use the cutlery from the outside in. (The kinds of cutlery you have indicates what will be served.)

3. Dessert cutlery is at the top of the place setting.

While Dining . . .

- Platters are received from the left and passed to the right. Waitstaff will serve from the left and remove from the right. When the waitstaff arrives to do this, do not look startled or discombobulated.

- Request items on the table rather than reaching over to retrieve them.

- While helping one diner pass food to another, do not take advantage of your position by helping yourself. That, as my grandma would have said, is piggish.

- Always pass the salt and pepper together as a set. They want to be together.

- Never season a dish before tasting it. If you see a tiny bowl and spoon of salt at your place setting, it is yours. But still don't season before you taste.

- Remember what your mother tried to tell you at the table: *chew with your mouth closed, speak only after swallowing, and never go for a second bite until the first bite is in your tummy.*

American or Continental?

Have you ever had a meal in another country and noticed that you and your American companions were the only ones who use the fork and knife in a "zig zag" kind of way? You are noticing a major variation in dining etiquette. The term "variation" might be misleading because only Americans vary cutlery technique from the International, or Continental style that the rest of the world uses.

How this variation came to be is the subject of great debate. All Europeans ate in the American style until sometime in the 1800s. One theory is that it began with a French etiquette expert, spread around the world, and never quite made it to our shores.

Nowadays, you do see Americans using the International style in restaurants in the U.S., but the pressure for you to use the International style doesn't squeeze until you travel. Then, you'll think back to the description below:

"American"
More methodical / requires discipline / noisy
Called "zig zag"
Knife in right hand, fork in left when cutting
Both held "pointer's knuckle-up" when cutting
Only one piece is cut at a time
Knife is placed at the top of the plate when not in use. Fork is then switched to the right hand with thumb over top of handle.

International or "Continental"
More efficient / graceful / quiet
Knife in right hand, fork in left while cutting AND while eating
Wrists lean on the edge of the table
Wrist pivots to a backhand-out position when bringing food to the mouth.

Practice, planning, and a bit of poise will give you a successful dining experience, but things can go wrong anyway. Below are some (if not all) of the possibilities.

If you make a mess of things . . .

- If you are late for the event, simply say "I'm sorry I'm late," rather than providing an extensive narrative or list of excuses.

- If you drop an object on the floor, leave it there and quietly ask the server for a replacement, if appropriate. If you dropped something personal like your phone, shame on you! (But discreetly retrieve it when you get up to leave at the end of the meal.)

- Whoops! An unexpected noise? Just say "excuse me" and act like nothing happened.

- When you feel a sneeze coming (hopefully, your mouth is empty) turn toward your left shoulder or inner elbow and sneeze into it. People notice when you sneeze into your hand and they will hesitate when called upon to shake it.

- Cover a cough with the inside of your arm and turn AWAY from the table.

- Blow your nose only in the restroom.

- When you need to leave for the restroom, simply stand up and say "excuse me." No need for a hall pass.

- If you are the hostess and the bill arrives at the table, ensure that you are the only one who can read it. (If you host a business dining event, arrange the payment ahead of time so the bill doesn't appear at the table.)

- If you are in no condition to drive, hand your keys to a friend and have him or her drive you home, or call for a ride. If you are alone with the host, excuse yourself to call a cab.

How to business network when food and alcohol are involved

- Anytime alcohol is involved, eat beforehand and then take as little alcohol as possible. (The rule is one drink or none!) No matter what's served at an event, eat a little food before you arrive so that you don't overindulge on food or so that a little bit of alcohol will not have an undue effect on you.

- Walk into the event with a purpose in mind. Look like you have this purpose.

- Check-in or register. Place your name tag on the right side of your jacket slightly above chest-level.

- Develop a great handshake with eye contact.

- Do not hover around the bar or food table.

- Take as little food onto any plate as possible.

- Despite what others are doing, this is not a time to flirt, talk trashy, or gossip.

EXCUSE ME BUT . . .

there's virtue in your manners.

I don't mean to give the impression that successfully living together depends only upon good manners. Heavens no! Living with others relies heavily on how we value others and view their purpose. It goes beyond manners and has to do with the personal virtue I talked about in Chapter 2. (Remember *Frog and Toad*?) Below is a list of goals with the corresponding "virtues." Some of these words you've heard in passing. Maybe you've wondered what they mean.

GOAL	VIRTUES (GOOD QUALITIES)	VICES (BAD STUFF)
See each and every person's true value and purpose; help them when necessary; show appropriate affection.	*Charity* (kindness, helpfulness), *love, justice* (fairness), *purity* (seeing the person as a person and not as an object for fun or material gain)	*Rudeness, meanness, hate, injustice, impurity*
Remain positive about others; smile when appropriate; don't gossip.	*Cheerfulness, justice*	*Meanness, cruelty, injustice*
Tell the truth even when it's difficult; place your name on the work only you have completed, pay your debts.	*Honesty* (being truthful), *sincerity* (a way of not being complicated about how you feel or what you think), *justice*	*Dishonesty, insincerity, injustice, cheating*
Do what you say you will do; **mean what you say**; keep your "word of honor."	*Sincerity, honesty, justice, courage*	*Insincerity, dishonesty, deceit, injustice, cowardice*

GOAL	VIRTUES (GOOD QUALITIES)	VICES (BAD STUFF)
Listen well to others; don't butt into their speaking time; wait without complaining; use manners (for the sake of others, not just for business or "getting ahead").	*Patience, justice, cheerfulness, kindness, graciousness* (helping someone feel welcomed, at home, and accepted)	*Impatience, injustice, grouchiness, sourpuss-ness, rudeness*
Eat and drink in healthy ways; get to bed on time; get to work on time; get to everything else on time so that others aren't inconvenienced; keep your stuff clean and organized.	*Temperance* (an old word for self-control), *punctuality, order*	*Intemperance, gluttony, laziness, inconsideration, disorder, sloppiness*
See your own true value and purpose; avoid boasting and bragging; give the appropriate person credit for something good; keep yourself clean and well-dressed without obsessing about it or comparing yourself to others.	*Humility, modesty* (a kind of humility, specifically a choice of fashions in clothing, speech, and interactions that affirm you as a person and not as an object), *justice*	*Arrogance, conceit, boastfulness, immodesty, injustice, vanity*
Apply rules evenly to people, even people you don't like; don't stereotype others, repeat bias, prejudice, or bigotry; defend the innocent; give friends the benefit of the doubt.	*Justice, loyalty*	*Injustice, cruelty*
Give help and time to those in need; give resources and money to those in need; avoid calculating costs to self; think big.	*Generosity, graciousness, magnanimity* (big-thinking generosity)	*Selfishness, stinginess, self centeredness, narcissism*

GOAL	VIRTUES (GOOD QUALITIES)	VICES (BAD STUFF)
Thank people when appropriate; **maintain a thankful attitude;** don't look out only for yourself.	*Thankfulness, gratitude, justice*	*Greed, rudeness, injustice*
Respect the property of others; don't "borrow" things without permission; don't steal or damage others' property.	*Respect, honesty, justice*	*Disrespect, dishonesty, thievery*
Work well even when you don't feel like it; complete work on time, change activity when needed (leaving screen-time, not wasting other people's time with nonsense, etc.).	*Fortitude* (stick with it-ness, going the extra mile), *industriousness* (Getting much quality work done in a specified amount of time)	*Laziness, injustice*
Struggle to do everything listed above, even when it's unpopular or people are teasing you about it.	*Fortitude, courage, justice*	*Weakness, cowardice, injustice*

The ancient Greeks (yes, those guys again), most major religions, and some of the greatest figures in history all agree that these virtues are needed by everyone to make the world go 'round smoothly. Virtue is what activates and maintains connections, communications, and understandings. Imagine if some of the nastiest people in history at least *tried* to live these standards. History may have unfolded differently.

How to enjoy a party
a place to test your virtue

1. Dress for it. Take into account that someone has gone to the trouble of planning, spending money, and working to make guests happy. Keep that in mind when you choose your party outfit.

2. Check your negativity at the door. Better yet, dissolve it completely with happy thoughts. Walk into a party with a smile and an open mind.

3. It's nice to take photos with a phone, but resist the urge to find more (or better) fun with your phone.

4. People first; food second. Greet friends and say hello to people you don't know before you hit the food table.

5. Limit your consumption of alcohol. Better yet, pour water into your opaque cup and sip all night. (I say *opaque* because people are nosy and always seem to be concerned that you are getting enough alcohol.) Either way, you'll feel better than anyone else by the end of the evening.

6. Focus on your conversation partner in the moment of conversation. Look him or her in the eyes and avoid looking around for more interesting conversations. Remember, he or she is a person with feelings and value too.

7. Have a goal to make at least one new friend at the party. A new friend is like a new treasure.[47]

---

47 I cannot end this section without thanking my mentor, Margery Sinclair, an international business etiquette consultant who really practices what she preaches. A good way to learn the specifics of etiquette (and to keep track of days that are important to the people you love) is to follow the book *A Year of Good Manners* by Margery and our mutual friend, the artist Jan Polk. Find it at www.margerysinclair.com.

When it's not a party, you'll need some order

Have you ever attended a meeting and heard things like, "I second the motion," or, "This meeting is adjourned"? If you haven't, you will, and you'll give yourself a great boost if you at least glance at *Robert's Rules of Order* so that you can get the gist of what's going on.

Henry Martyn Robert *(May 2, 1837–May 11, 1923) was horribly embarrassed to have performed badly while presiding over a public meeting. He vowed to learn what's called "parliamentary procedure" and eventually wrote the book we now call* Robert's Rules of Order, *which became the most widely used manual of parliamentary procedure. Today, in its eleventh edition, it remains the most common parliamentary authority in the United States. Companies, clubs, boards, and committees use these rules when meeting officially.*

I DO FOR YOU!

With all those etiquette books specifically written for weddings, you'd think we wouldn't have been able to produce a show called "*Bridezilla.*" (Or, maybe that's why we do have this show!)[48] Anyway,

---

[48] The issue resembles the old question of "which came first the chicken or the egg?" With so much attention being paid to brides through the ages, I suppose we've created this monster.

no book on communication should ever leave out the topics of marriage and weddings. The connection-communication-understanding cycle between a man and a woman can become one of the most wonderful relationships on the planet, and so it should begin with a well-mannered shindig.

Then, long after the wedding, husband and wife must continually attend to the cycle of connection-communication-understanding for the rest of their lives. Although it can be daunting to think about the effort that goes into making marriage work, don't be intimidated; if you do it right, it will be a wonderful and even exciting adventure!

So, what does a woman preparing for a wedding need to know? Two things (mainly):

1. She needs to know that the wedding is not about the bride. It's about the bride and groom, the family, the community, and all the generations before us. (Coordinating the bridesmaids' dresses to the bridal bouquet suddenly doesn't seem so important after all.)

2. She needs to know that marriage is a gift we've inherited from all the generations preceding us. It is indeed a exhilarating union unlike any other, and it has been entrusted to us to pass on to the next generations preserved and undamaged.

The five fundamentals for choosing a wedding dress[49]

1. Your dress should be representative of this gift (marriage) you've inherited from generations before you. It should be formal and dignified.

2. The dress should be worthy of you. It shouldn't provide competing focal points such as cleavage or skin lumping around the armholes.

3. White or ivory? White works best for women who need a cool palette and ivory works best for women who need a warm palette.

4. If it's impossible to find a dress that reflects your muse (or you are wearing an older relative's dress), inject your personality into an accessory or your bouquet. Wear shoes you can handle. (Not flip-flops, please.)

5. Put together your look with grace. Hold your head high, walk like a lady, and smile.

---

49 A new trend for buying the bridal gown is to visit secondhand venues which specialize in serving the bridal party in an elegant boutique and with skilled service. One venue, Cherie Amour, provides the most breathtaking setting for this big decision and its proceeds fund *Success In Style*'s studios throughout Maryland. (www.successinstyle.org)

THE BIG GIG

revisited

Communication situations that require personal virtue go well beyond weddings, formal banquets, parliamentary proceedings, or dates. You could argue that the day-to-day interactions among family members, friends, or people in our neighborhoods require even more effort because, when faced with the ordinary, we may be tempted to "let down our hair" and just "be who we are."

There's an expression: *character is doing the right thing even when no one is looking.*[50] This expression calls to mind the character it takes to be at our best even when we are among people who will love us no matter what. After all, when we are sleepy, weary, or unsociable, we are still likely to be called upon to connect with another person, and even then we should be at our best and most loving because very likely at those times we're connecting with the people we love the most.

SO NOW OUR RELATIONSHIP COMES TO AN END

with six parting points

At the beginning of this book, I suggested that your total communication is made up of different channels, and that the best

---

50 In the U.S., the quote is generally attributed to African–American former U.S. Representative Julius Caesar (J.C.) Watts, but there are many older variations of this saying.

communications uses all of these channels to promote understanding and build relationships. The message of this book is essentially the following:

- Hold your head up high because you know your great value.

- Work with the knowledge of your true purpose.

- Listen to others; they have value and purpose—and something to say.

- Dress according to your great dignity as a woman.

- Consume media and leave your mark in the world is a way that is worthy of your dignity.

- Live virtue and practice social graces.

Understanding in a World of Misunderstanding

As you've learned, friendship is the good and beautiful process of understanding the *other*. Some friendships make discovering the mystery of the other fun, while other friendships entail more of a struggle. Although you might be tempted to value the more difficult friendship less, there is merit in the struggle to understand the person who doesn't make it easy for us (as long as the relationship is a healthy one).

Often, you hear people say "no one understands me," or "hopefully one day you'll understand," so you wonder if some people are just doomed to being misunderstood. Generally, however, no one is completely isolated in this way. In fact, others might understand the situation well enough not to agree with the person's choices about what she considers to be misunderstood.

For example, let's say that a kleptomaniac (a person with a compulsion to steal randomly) feels that no one understands her as a kleptomaniac. Yes, the people in her life do know about her random stealing. They agree with the diagnosis of "kleptomaniac" and are trying to sympathize with hardships imposed by such a condition. They just do not condone the choices surrounding the label. *They refuse to give her permission to steal.* That refusal could cause consternation for someone who feels she needs affirmation in "who she is," even if it's something she shouldn't be.

We've been conditioned to think that because someone doesn't condone the actions we've justified by our own thought processes, we are misunderstood. This belief distorts the real meaning of "understanding." We can grow and improve ourselves when we learn to know the difference between understanding and condoning, concurring, or enabling.

CAN WE EVER TOTALLY AND COMPLETELY UNDERSTAND ANOTHER PERSON?

Despite everything I've said up to this point, the answer is *no.* And no other person can totally and completely understand you either. Don't be too amazed by this answer, though. If you pause for a moment to recall the first chapter, you'll find good reasoning for this answer in our discussion on your value and purpose.

A very special friend who loves you understands you a lot, but not completely. You feel his or her love and concern, which bolsters your sense of value and purpose. You must admit, however, that there's a gap in your soul that never seems to be filled despite the kindest, nicest, most loving act of another human heart. You are continually craving something more, something greater. The truth is that there is no one thing, or even person, in this world who can fill it.

Remember the Source of all that is beautiful and good and

true? He's the source of all the understanding you've received and will receive across your lifetime. He is also the one and only source who understands you totally, completely, and absolutely. That gap in your soul has a corresponding satisfaction, just as food satisfies hunger, drink satisfies thirst, or warmth satisfies cold. This ultimate satisfaction is the truest, deepest, and most complete kind of satisfaction there is, and it goes well beyond physical or even emotional fulfillment. It follows that only the truest, deepest, and most complete source can meet this need: God, your Creator.

Sources and Suggestions for Further Reading

Ammer, Chirstine. *The American Heritage Dictionary of Idioms: American English Idiomatic Expressions and Phrases (Second Edition)*. Rockville, MD: American Heritage Inc., 2011.

Austen, Jane. *Complete and Unabridged (Sense and Sensibility, Pride and Prejudice, Mansfield Park, Emma, Northanger Abbey, Persuasion, Lady Susan)*. New York: Midpoint Press, 2006.

Bennet, Art, Bennet, Laraine. *The Temperament God Gave You: The Classic Key to Knowing Yourself, Getting Along with Others and Growing Closer to the Lord*. Manchester, NH: Sophia Institute Press, 2005.

Bluedorn, Nathaniel, Bluedorn, Hans, *The Fallacy Detective: Thirty-eight Lessons on How to Recognize Bad Reasoning*, 2008.

Campbell, Collin. "The Modern Western Fashion Pattern, its Functions and Relationship to Identity." *Fashion and Identity*, edited by Gonzalez, A.M. Bovone, L. NY: Social Trends Institute, 2007.

Cline, Elizabeth. *Overdressed: The Shockingly High Cost of Cheap Fashion*. New York: Penguin, 2012.

Douglass, Frederick. *Narrative of the Life of Frederick Douglass*. New York: Millennium Publications, 2014.

Frankl, Victor E. *Man's Search for Meaning*. Boston, MA: Beacon, 1959.

Gibson, William. *The Miracle Worker*. New York: Scribner, 1956.

Hollander, Anne. *Sex and Suits: The Evolution of Modern Dress*. New York: Kodansha, 1994.

Ilibagiza, Immaculee. *Left to Tell: Discovering God Amidst the Rwandan Holocaust*. New York: Hay House, 2006.

John Paul II. *The Theology of the Body: Human Love in the Divine Plan*. Boston: Pauline Books and Media, 1997.

Jones, Susan Jenkyn. *Fashion Design*. London: Lawrence King Publishing, 2011.

Kreeft, Peter. *You Can Understand the Bible: A Practical and Illuminating Guide to Each Book in the Bible*. San Francisco, CA: Ignatius, 2005.

Lobel, Arnold. *Frog and Toad are Friends*. New York: Harper Collins, 1970.

Robert, Henry. *Robert's Rules of Order, Newly Revised*. Philadelphia, PA: Da Capo Press, 2011.

Rock, David. *Your Brain at Work: Strategies for Overcoming Distraction, Regaining Focus, and Working Smarter All Day Long.* New York: Harper Collins, 2009.

Sinclair, M. Polk, J. *A Year of Good Manners.* 2008

Stowe, Harriet Beecher. *Uncle Tom's Cabin; or, Life Among the Lowly.* New York: Random House, 1996.

Strunk, William, White, E.B. *The Elements of Style (Fourth Edition).* Harlow, Essex, UK: Pearson Education Limited, 2014.

Ten Boom, Corrie. *The Hiding Place (25th Anniversary Edition).* Grand Rapids, MI: Chosen Books, 2001.

The Navarre Bible: New Testament Expanded Edition. New York: Four Courts / Scepter, 2008.

Turkle, Sherry. *Reclaiming Conversation: The Power of Talk in a Digital Age.* New York: Penguin Random House, 2016

Wattenberg, Laura. *The Baby Name Wizard: A Magical Method for Finding the Perfect Name for Your Baby.* New York: Three Rivers Press, 2013.

Warren, Mary Sheehan. *It's So You! Fitting Fashion to Your Life.* New York: Scepter: 2011.

SUGGESTED WEBSITES:

Personal Fashion

www.successinstyle.org (An organization which helps others)

www.fashionintelligence.org.

www.verilymag.com (Fashion and lifestyle)

www.darlingmagazine.org (Fashion and lifestyle)

https://www.youtube.com/watch?v=-WlqBjKC0C8 (RacchLoves' Makeup Tutorial using different and more involved techniques from the one in this book)

Language

https://www.merriam-webster.com/words-at-play/eggcorn-meaning-and-examples (Fun to read!)

www.toastmasters.org (Includes tips and videos)

Manners

www.margerysinclair.com

https://www.youtube.com/watch?v=HDTB7jsc0UY, (Youtube video created for the fellows, but it's the best tutorial out there!)

Photo Credits

(In order of appearance)

Montse Grases, Archivo Fotográfico de la Oficina de Información del Opus Dei en Internet - https://www.flickr.com/photos/opus-dei/16678996444/

Letty Bowman, used with permission from her son, William Bowman.

Christina Sheehan and Christina and Joseph Sheehan, from the author's own collection.

The Hope Diamond, National Museum of Natural History. Public domain via Wikimedia Commons.

Immaculee Ilibagiza, used with permission, https://www.immaculee.com/

Daguerreotype of Frederick Douglass 1847-52, Art Institute of Chicago [Public domain], via Wikimedia Commons.

Virgin and Child with Balaam the Prophet, Catacomb of Priscilla. Public domain via Wikimedia Commons.

Joe and Rosemary Sheehan (undated), from author's own collection

Irena Sendler, Unknown, Teresa Prekerowa "Konspiracyjna Rada Pomocy Żydom w Warszawie 1942-1945"(The underground Council to Aid Jews in Warsaw 1942-1945) Warszawa 1982. Public domain via Wikimedia Commons.

Irena Sendler in 2005, By Mariusz Kubik, http://www.mariuszkubik.pl. Public domain via Wikimedia Commons.

Joe and Rosemary Sheehan (undated), from author's own collection

Edith Stein, HI. Teresia Benedicta vom Kreuz, 1920; Unknown - Ökumenisches Heiligenlexiko. Public domain via Wikimedia Commons.

Jane Austen, Cropped from Image: Jane Austen 1870.jpg. 1869 engraving showing an idealized, young en:Jane Austen, based on a sketch by Cassandra Austen. Public domain via Wikimedia Commons.

Sojourner Truth, By Randall Studio (National Portrait Gallery, Smithsonian Institution). Public domain via Wikimedia Commons.

Old engraved illustration of a Common Toad. Trousset Encyclopedia. Morphart Creation / Shutterstock

Helen Keller, Public domain via Wikimedia Commons.

Socks with sandals. Dirk Ott / Shutterstock.

Elizabeth I by Crsipin van dee Passe after Isaac Oliver. Public domain via Wikimedia Commons.

Detail of 15th century illuminated manuscript, Renaud de Montauban banquet. Public domain via Wikimedia Commons.

Philip Dawe Public domain, via Wikimedia Commons.

By English: Pietro Antonio Martini [(1738–1797) engraver] after Jean-Michel Moreau the Younger [(1741–1814). Public domain, via Wikimedia Commons.

By Drawn by Pauqet for Petit Courrier des Dames. Public domain, via Wikimedia Commons.

Thorax – Venus de Milo and mannequin, vintage illustrations from Die Frau als Hausarztin 1911, Shutterstock.

Royal Worcester Bon Ton Corsets. Public domain via Wikimedia Commons.

Victorian corset, public domain via Wikimedia Commons.

From compendium of Christine de Pizan's works, 1413. Produced in her scriptorium in Paris. Public domain via Wikimedia Commons.

American fashion designer Claire McCardell surrounded by models wearing her designs., Time Magazine, May 2, 1955, public domain via Wikimedia Commons

Joe and Rosemary Sheehan (undated photo) from author's own collection

Fashion designer Carolina Herrera celebrating Ralph Lauren's 40th Anniversary at the Conservancy Garden, Central Park, New York City, Photo by Christopher Peterson. Public domain via Wikimedia Commons.

Press release publicity photo of Ingrid Bergman for film *Gaslight* (1944), public domain via Wikimedia Commons.

By Archives New Zealand from New Zealand ("Happy Valentine's Day"). Public domain via Wikimedia Commons.

Cursive letters. Baksiabat / Shutterstock.

Portrait of Harriet Beecher Stowe By Francis Holl (1815–1884) after George Richmond (28 March 1809 – 19 March 1896). Public domain via Wikimedia Commons.

Anne Frank, By Unknown photographer; Collectie Anne Frank Stichting Amsterdam (Website Anne Frank Stichting, Amsterdam). Public domain via Wikimedia Commons.

Saint Margaret of Scotland, icon by Marice. Used with permission. http://www.iconsbymarice.com.au/

Henry Martyn Robert. Public domain via Wikimedia Commons.

About the Author

Mary Sheehan Warren currently teaches Consumer Behavior and Fashion Marketing at the Busch School of Business at the Catholic University of America. Mary has twenty-two years of experience as a social entrepreneur. She founded a Maryland-based non-profit organiza-  tion dedicated to professional presence training (now called Success In Style), personally training hundreds of women from dozens of organizations across three continents to continue its mission in their respective locations. Currently, she is leading the Fashion Intelligence Project, an organization dedicated to human dignity and sustainable fashion consumption.

Upon the publication of her book, *It's So You! Fitting Fashion to Your Life* (Spence Publishing, 2007), Mary began her own consulting business, ISYFashion, in Milwaukee, Wisconsin, working especially with businesses, professional organizations, universities, and individuals on professional development, personal branding, and general fashion education. She now works with Success In Style in the Washington, DC area and lives in Springfield, Virginia with her husband, Robert, and their five children.